Susan?

Praise for

...eart Wide Open

"*Heart Wide Open* will fuel your desire for a deeper relationship with God and give you the gentle nudge and the steps to get it. So much of this book spoke to me that I had to get out my highlighter pen! Wherever you are in your faith, you will benefit from reading of Shellie's journey to a deeper, stronger, more intimate relationship with our Creator. She tells it like it is, with love, good humor, and abandon, as she writes out of an honest and open love for God, for His Word, and for you! With every word you read, you can sense her excitement as she went through this journey, and it will tug on your heart, calling you to join her in falling in love with Jesus all over again."

—KORIE ROBERTSON of A&E's *Duck Dynasty*

"Shellie Rushing Tomlinson writes with wit, wisdom, and plain-spoken truth. She throws open the doors and calls women to step into a deeper, wider, more soul-fulfilling love for Scripture, for themselves, and for the Lord. *Heart Wide Open* reads like a conversation with a best girlfriend and a wise mentor, all in one."

—LISA WINGATE, national best-selling author of *The Prayer Box*

"Fans who love Shellie for her fabulous sense of humor will have their hearts warmed by her emotional vulnerability in these pages. She dives deep into her personal faith journey, sharing her own search for a genuine relationship with Christ. For everyone who longs to have an intimate bond with their Savior, this book will teach you to live with your heart wide open."

—JULIE CANTRELL, *New York Times* best-selling author of *Into the Free*

"In *Heart Wide Open,* Shellie Tomlinson shares the beauty of her heart and the journey she took to trade a mundane faith for the abundant life with Jesus we have all been invited to. She does it in her southern and inviting way, wrapped up in her gift of storytelling, while still challenging the reader's heart to dive into the deep topics of our obedience, prayer, and courage."

—DENISE HILDRETH JONES, author of *Reclaiming Your Heart*

"I know two things about Shellie Tomlinson without question: she is an incredibly gifted storyteller with a sense of humor that never fails to save me from despair, and she is a true woman of deep and abiding faith. What I didn't know until now is that she is able to use both those qualities to teach us how to embrace an intimate relationship with God. In *Heart Wide Open* she has made me laugh aloud one moment and then be moved with the wisdom of her words at the next line. Shellie shows us how to take the two great commandments—to love God with all our hearts and to love our neighbors as ourselves—and integrate those things into the perfume of our everyday lives. Regardless of how long you have been on your faith journey, you will discover wisdom in these pages that will draw you closer to God and show you how to love His people with more patience. And, my friends, at the close of the day that is what it's all about."

—RIVER JORDAN, author of *Praying for Strangers*

"This book pushes me to be more vulnerable to the Father who loves me more than my own family—and that's a lot. How wonderful to know that God not only loves us for who we are, but that He created us the way He wants us. He wants us to pour our lives out to Him to glorify Him. Thank you, Shellie, for encouraging us all through this book to draw closer to our God and to keep our hearts wide open to all the possibilities He has for us!"

—MISSY ROBERTSON of A&E's *Duck Dynasty*

"So many of us have a longing for more in our Christian lives. In *Heart Wide Open*, Shellie Rushing Tomlinson fans this flame within us as she points our hearts toward a life of joy, excitement, and wonder in God. Her words will wrap around you like a hug, and you'll find yourself being equipped to engage in your daily relationship with the Lord like never before."

—LISA BEVERE, best-selling author of *Girls with Swords* and *Lioness Arising*

"To read Shellie Rushing Tomlinson is to make a new friend. Her writing is filled with sound theology, great insight, humor, and authenticity. I recommend this book to all who want to draw closer to Jesus. Her questions for Bible study are thought provoking and ripe for discussions. I have no doubt this study will strike a chord for many and be a great tool for personal spiritual growth."

—PAMELA GREGG FOXWORTHY, wife of comedian Jeff Foxworthy

"I love Shellie Tomlinson's humor, but it's her heart that I most want to listen to. I'm so glad she's chosen to share it in *Heart Wide Open*. This is the book I've wanted her to write, filled with her unique blend of realness and wisdom."

—MARYBETH WHALEN, author of *The Bridge Tender* and cofounder of She Reads

"This is a charming, funny, honest, touching look at one southern woman's journey to a profound relationship with Christ. As the title suggests, Shellie lives with her heart wide open to the questions, the mysteries, and the certainties of our faith. You will love this book!"

—SHEILA WALSH, author of *The Storm Inside*

"Shellie Rushing Tomlinson gets to the heart of everyday faith in *Heart Wide Open* with her signature storytelling and wit, opening her own heart to share about learning to walk with God. Her use of life lessons mingled with Scripture is sure to capture the heart of every believer and every seeking soul."

—RACHEL HAUCK, award-winning author of *Once Upon a Prince*

"My Kentucky mamaw told me I was 'as handy as a pocket in a shirt.' Southern women just know how to turn a phrase and a head, which is why you won't want to miss Shellie's down-home, upbeat take on life, seen through cool drafts of sweet tea and sass. My favorite way to learn is to laugh myself sane. Thanks, Shellie."

—PATSY CLAIRMONT, author of *Twirl: A Fresh Spin at Life*

HEART WIDE OPEN

TRADING MUNDANE FAITH
FOR AN EXUBERANT LIFE WITH JESUS

SHELLIE RUSHING TOMLINSON

WATERBROOK
PRESS

Heart Wide Open

All Scripture quotations, unless otherwise indicated, are taken from the New American Standard Bible®. © Copyright The Lockman Foundation 1960, 1962, 1963, 1968, 1971, 1972, 1973, 1975, 1977, 1995. Used by permission. (www.Lockman.org). Scripture quotations marked (AMP) are taken from the Amplified Bible. Copyright © 1954, 1958, 1962, 1964, 1965, 1987 by The Lockman Foundation. Used by permission. Scripture quotations marked (ASV) are taken from the American Standard Version. Scripture quotations marked (HCSB) are taken from The Holman Christian Standard Bible®, © copyright 1999, 2000, 2002, 2003 by Holman Bible Publishers. Used by permission. Scripture quotations marked (NIV) are taken from the Holy Bible, New International Version®, NIV®. Copyright © 1973, 1978, 1984 by Biblica Inc.™ Used by permission of Zondervan. All rights reserved worldwide. www.zondervan.com. Scripture quotations marked (NKJV) are taken from the New King James Version®. Copyright © 1982 by Thomas Nelson Inc. Used by permission. All rights reserved.

Trade Paperback ISBN 978-0-307-73193-7
eBook ISBN 978-0-307-73194-4

Copyright © 2014 by Shellie Tomlinson

Cover design by Kelly L. Howard

Published in the United States by WaterBrook, an imprint of the Crown Publishing Group, a division of Penguin Random House LLC, New York.

WATERBROOK® and its deer colophon are registered trademarks of Penguin Random House LLC.

Library of Congress Cataloging-in-Publication Data
Tomlinson, Shellie Rushing.
    Heart wide open : trading mundane faith for an exuberant life with Jesus / Shellie Rushing Tomlinson.—
First Edition.
       pages cm
    Includes bibliographical references.
    ISBN 978-0-307-73193-7—ISBN 978-0-307-73194-4 1. Christian life. 2. Spiritual life—Christianity.
I. Title.
    BV4501.3.T658 2014
    248.4—dc23

                                              2013035983

Printed in the United States of America
2018

10 9 8 7 6 5 4

SPECIAL SALES
Most WaterBrook books are available at special quantity discounts when purchased in bulk by corporations, organizations, and special-interest groups. Custom imprinting or excerpting can also be done to fit special needs. For information, please e-mail specialmarketscms@penguinrandomhouse.com or call 1-800-603-7051.

To Phil, love of my life and sharer of the dream

CONTENTS

Contents

1

WHEN ALL YOU CAN BRING HIM
IS A BROKEN WANT-TO

*"Jesus, I know I don't love You like I
should, but I want to want to love You!"*

I like to say I was in church nine months before I was born and shortly thereafter my people began toting me back to the Lord's house as quickly and as often as they could. I now understand there are worse places to grow up than the left side, second row of a small country church, but as a rambunctious kid with a serious imagination and a bad case of the fidgets, I had a hard time imagining why so much churchgoing was necessary.

It seemed highly unlikely we would miss out on anything earth shattering if we skipped a service here and there. Even a wiggly little tomboy with smudged eyeglasses could tell you who was going to come in late, who was going to make a scene taking her baby to the nursery, and which elderly deacon was going to rouse himself from a brief nap to offer a hearty "Amen!" People are creatures of habit even—and maybe especially—in the Lord's house.

To my way of thinking, a little absence could have made our much-churched hearts grow even fonder. My sisters concurred. Had this ever come to a vote, we girls would have ruled the day with a three-to-two tally, but our parents weren't the least bit interested in running a democracy.

Our list of required appearances included, but was not limited to, Sunday morning, Sunday night, Wednesday night, two-week vacation Bible schools in the summer, and two-week annual revivals in the spring and fall, both revivals having been prefaced with two-week cottage prayer meetings in anticipation of the big events. Sickness could get you an excused absence from any of these services, but it had to be verified. Holding a thermometer inside your electric blanket so you could stay home on Sunday night and watch *The Wonderful World of Disney* never worked. Not that I ever tried.

As a child, I enjoyed the rhythm of familiar hymns as well as the sense of belonging I felt inside those church walls, even if I firmly believed we overdid the whole attendance thing. As a teenager, however, I became increasingly skilled at being present in body alone while my thoughts were occupied elsewhere with my peers and our many dramas. I had a healthy respect for the teachings of the church, and God seemed real enough to me while I was there, but I didn't understand why my faith felt so compartmentalized. Where God went once I left the church building I couldn't say. And honestly, I wasn't all that concerned with the mystery.

This disconnect between my Sunday morning faith and my everyday experience followed me into my young married life where, despite my childhood conclusion that our parents overdid the churching, I found myself choosing the same level of commitment to the weekly services. I still enjoyed attending church, but I could seldom carry the warm fuzzies I felt during the service any farther than the parking lot before my sense of God's presence began to fade. The Sundays that bookended my weeks seemed to have little to do with what happened in the days that lay between them. As the years rolled by, I gradually began to wonder why this was and if it had to be. Thankfully, the day finally came when I was ready to admit that I needed something more. I had no clue what it was that had been missing for so long, yet I knew I had to find it.

As it happens, God used my own children to turn up the heat under my growing desire for more. I was a married woman with a loving husband trying to raise two young teenagers when the persistent dissatisfaction I'd never been able to name began to reach a boiling point.

During my kids' early years, I'd been able to pull off the church-lady gig, or at least my concept of the role. I knew the Bible and I knew the rules. Thinking this would be enough, I forged ahead, confident that if my husband and I took our children to church every time the doors opened, just as my parents had done with my sisters and me, all would be well. And for the most part it was—until they hit adolescence and I came down with mommy terrors!

> I had no clue what it was that
> had been missing for so long,
> yet I knew I had to find it.

My babies were growing up, and it was both exhilarating and terrifying. Everywhere I turned the culture around us was laughing at what I considered sacred and celebrating what I found immoral. Increasingly our kids were exposed to things outside our home that neither their dad nor I approved of, and it frightened me to realize the temptations they faced could potentially wreck the futures we had always dreamed of for them. I tried to placate myself. We had taught them our values. If they were strong in their faith, they would be okay come what may, right? I had already purchased this holy life insurance myself, hadn't I? I simply needed to make sure they had taken out a similar policy. I needed to know they believed me when I said that the fullest life was one lived in God.

Such logic should have brought peace, and it would have, if not for one overgrown, peanut-eating elephant loafing smack-dab in the middle of my living room: I had zero life experience to offer as evidence for what I was advertising. As much as I disliked admitting it, any spiritual direction I was offering my kids came strictly from the biblical head knowledge gained through my years in the pew. I was merely regurgitating what I'd heard my whole life.

In short, I was a hypocrite!

Though the news came as quite a surprise to me, the ugly truth was undeniable. An Internet dictionary offers the following spot-on definition of my true state in that telling moment: a hypocrite is "a person who pretends to have virtues, moral or religious beliefs, principles, etc., that he or she does not actually possess, especially a person whose actions belie stated beliefs."[1]

Bingo. If I were to be honest, the faith I was experiencing wasn't satisfying my deepest longings at all. My picture could've been pasted right beside that entry. Say "cheese," Church Lady.

Even as I came face to face with the realization that I couldn't pass on something I didn't have, I was also painfully aware that young people are like mini lie detectors, capable of spotting anything short of the whole truth and willing to call you on it. I'm reminded of the time I came through the living room all dressed up for a big event, whereupon my grade school son looked up and announced, "Wow, Mama. You do not look fat in those pants." Obviously, Phillip had heard this subject discussed in his few short years on earth, and, just as clearly, there had been other times when I had looked fat in my pants. But enough of *What Not to Wear*. My point is, children can sniff out insincerity like a bloodhound and see through hypocrites with their eyes closed. My Big Faith Advertisement must have sounded as weak in their ears as it did in mine.

This sobering realization about the lameness of my own faith stared me down without blinking and prompted some serious soul searching. Why wasn't my faith satisfying? Why was it that my God and I were friendly acquaintances at best? Why didn't I know this One I called my Savior? Worse yet, *why didn't I love Him*? Oh, I liked Him well enough. I appreciated the gospel, and I was grateful for the promise of a secure eternity, but love this Jesus in the here and now? Not really. In light of all my years of churching and being churched, I wondered how on earth that could be true. And why did some people seem so passionate about Jesus when all I could muster for Him on my most spiritual day was a healthy respect?

I knew people who talked about Jesus with the kind of affection normally reserved for a flesh-and-blood person. Me? I could sing "Oh, how I love Jesus" as heartily as everyone around me (albeit off-key), but deep down I knew that I could just as easily be singing "Oh, how I love watermelon" for all the fervency in my aching faking heart. My fellow southerners and I have a saying we're fond of using to encourage someone to be honest. "Tell the truth and stay in church," we'll warn. I've always thought the line was funny, but I wasn't laughing as I compared my empty profession of love with the words of Jesus Himself in Mark 12:30: "Love the Lord your God with all your heart and with all your soul and with all your mind and with all your strength" (NIV). I knew I didn't love Him that way, and I didn't have the slightest idea what to do about it. Coming clean with my Jesus-loving church members about the state of my faith didn't sound at all appealing.

Have mercy! If this was all I had to advertise for my abundant life, I realized I was going to have a hard time selling God to my kids, or to anyone else for that matter.

FLYPAPER FAITH

With that, the nagging concern over my lackluster faith that had dogged me for years became a desperate need to find out what I was missing. I was no longer willing to settle for the distance that separated me from the God I'd heard about and prayed to from my earliest memory. I think of that turning point as my Flypaper Epiphany.

When I was growing up, most everyone I knew used flypaper to combat the bothersome insects that populate our southern summers. Flypaper seems to have lost its appeal over the years. But back in the day, these sticky pieces of vertical yellow tape, each about a foot and a half long and a couple inches wide, hung beneath carports all over our Louisiana Delta and as near as possible to the main entrances of our houses.

Flypaper is coated with sweet-smelling glue and designed to be so sticky that should a pesky fly encounter it while heading into the house, said insect would be immediately detained and permanently affixed to its surface. I can assure you that flypaper lives up to the billing. I once got my hair caught on the stuff, and I thought for sure Mama was going to have to shave me bald-headed to remove it from my crowning glory.

> Eternal life isn't a gift from God;
> eternal life is the gift of God.
> —Oswald Chambers

I don't remember the exact day I sat staring at John 17:3 (I do know it was shortly after I identified myself as a hypocrite), but I'll always remember the challenge I heard in Jesus's own words: "This is eternal life, that they might know You, the only true God, and Jesus Christ whom You have sent." That scripture was familiar to this church girl, but the hope I heard in it was brand spanking new. For the first time I saw in those words a way to get off the spiritual merry-go-round I'd been riding my whole life and strike out on the biggest adventure of all time: to actually know God. I saw this as the way I would learn to love Jesus, to crazy love Him.

In my new plan God was the flypaper, and I would be the fly. The mission: to throw myself at Him and stick for eternity! The rest of my life began with a single prayer and an honest admission that surprised neither of us:

"I admit it. I don't love You like I should, but I want to love You. Help!"

CHOOSING TO LOVE JESUS

I finally admitted that I had nothing to offer God. Zero. Zip. All I could bring was my weak, broken want-to. Here's the beautiful reality: it was enough. If you want to love Jesus, it's enough for you too!

The embarrassing truth I had avoided all my life—that I didn't really love Jesus—was the very admission He would use to ignite my lukewarm heart. Who knew?! All I had to offer was a desire to love Him, but it was enough. Okay, to be accurate, I couldn't even say that I wanted to love Him. It was more like I wanted to want to love Him, and still it was enough. He accepted my passionless heart and began to breathe on it, and a new way of living began opening to me.

I've had so many women tell me personal stories about their faith, and I'm always struck by how similar they are to my own. These sincere believers believe in God and they're trying to follow Him, but they admit to having little to no sense of intimacy with Him. They long for the passion they see in the Bible, but they're resigned to going through the motions without it. If this resonates with you, if you've been trying to ignore a certain dullness to your faith, please hear me. You aren't asking for anything that God doesn't want you to enjoy and Jesus didn't die to give you! I'm walking proof that you can fall in love with Jesus by learning to whisper a simple prayer that meets with His wholehearted approval: *"I don't love You, but I want to love You. Help me!"*

Taste the sugar-sweet words of Ephesians 1:3–4: "Blessed be the God and Father of our Lord Jesus Christ, who has blessed us with every spiritual blessing in the heavenly places in Christ, just as He chose us in Him before the foundation of the world."

God chose to love all of us, but He gave us free will to decide whether or not we would return that love. The type of honest prayer I'm advocating means admitting that our want-to is broken and asking God to teach us how to love Him well.

Have you been waiting for your heart to spontaneously combust into love for Jesus? If so, you have your cart before your horse, and I'm here to testify through firsthand experience that it's a frustrating way to ride and produces scant forward progress. In 1 John 4:19 we're told that "we love, because He first loved us." In other words, you and I will never be able to bear down and deliver a passionate heart for God out of determination or self-discipline, and it won't overtake us by surprise. It will, however, ignite in our hearts when we discover the secret of feasting on God's love in the person of Jesus Christ. Scripture assures us that He loves us not because of who we are but because of who He is.

But when the kindness of God our Savior and His love for mankind appeared, He saved us, not on the basis of deeds which we have done in righteousness, but according to His mercy, by the washing of regeneration and renewing by the Holy Spirit, whom He poured out upon us richly through Jesus Christ our Savior, so that being justified by His grace we would be made heirs according to the hope of eternal life. (Titus 3:4–7)

God put His love on eternal display by sending Jesus to save us, not because of our merit but in spite of our sin. He initiates the love affair with us. The blessed challenge is to continue drinking that love in as freely as we first reached for salvation. When we feast on this extravagant love and the many gifts He poured out upon us through Jesus Christ, we receive a nutrient-rich meal that nourishes His passion in us. But I reiterate, it is a decision, just as surely as the one we make when we pull our chairs up to the dining room table. No one can make this choice for us.

So what does this decision look like? That's the question I'm excited about answering. Let's begin with some powerful words from Jesus, recorded in Matthew.

Don't collect for yourselves treasures on earth, where moth and rust destroy and where thieves break in and steal. But collect for yourselves treasures in heaven, where neither moth nor rust destroys, and where thieves don't break in and steal. For where your treasure is, there your heart will be also. (6:19–21, HCSB)

For the longest time I allowed the good news of this passage to be totally eclipsed by the last sentence: "For where your treasure is, there your heart will be also." That sounded like something of a spiritual inkblot test to me, and it was one I was sure I could never pass. I was quite convinced that if God examined what it was I treasured, He would see that He wasn't at the top of the list. In my guilt-induced anxiety, I completely missed the clear directive of the passage. These six power-packed words turned my perceived inkblot test on its head when I finally understood their decree: "Collect for yourselves treasures in heaven." That, my friend, isn't a question or a suggestion. It's an instruction that begs a proactive, determined choice of action. It's also good news, foot-stomping good news. You and I get to choose what we treasure!

This power-packed privilege of choosing God as my treasure is the very decision I made on the day of my Flypaper Epiphany! I've since come to better understand the paradigm shift that occurred that day, but at the time I had no idea of the magnitude of my newly adjusted aim. I couldn't have known that the decision to toss aside all reserve and throw myself at God with the sole goal of coming to know Him would not only open the door to the passion I was missing but also rescue me from another of my persistent struggles.

THE PROBLEM WITH DR. SEUSS PRAYERS

For as long as I could remember, I had struggled to feel secure in my salvation. I knew what the Bible taught on the subject, but because my heart could find no rest, I had long followed the Dr. Seuss method in search of that elusive certainty that I belonged to God. Every altar call aggravated the inward struggle, so…

I prayed the sinner's prayer in a car. I prayed it near and I
     prayed it far.
I prayed it in a tree. I prayed it on bent knee.
I prayed it once for all, and I prayed it each time I heard
     an altar call.

The wonderful news is that when my focus changed from trying to know if I was saved to knowing the God who saved me, He began to lead me out of the endless frustration of not knowing if I belonged to Him and into an endless pursuit and delightful discovery of Him! Knowing that I am His and He is mine has brought a rest to my soul that trumps anything this world can offer.

I've since come to understand something else about those Dr. Seuss prayers. All of those earlier repetitious rituals were simply my confused responses to Christ's ongoing invitation to live in and through Him.

All those times I heard Jesus say, "Come unto Me," I thought He was inviting me to confirm my eternal destiny, when in reality I was hearing my Redeemer calling me to experience His presence. I had called on God one hundred and one times for salvation, while Christ called one hundred and two times for me to abide in Him, to do life in Him. He was and is forevermore constantly and consistently calling me to come to Him for life itself!

All those times I struggled to know if I was saved, that tug on my heart was Jesus calling me to come and discover the life God was offering me through Him, to come and find nourishment for my soul through Him, to come and rest through Him, to come and learn through Him. He hasn't stopped. He is calling you too. He is calling us right now to run to Him for our very lives. Come. Jesus doesn't ask us to come to Him just once, for salvation. Listen to His words in John 6:35: "I am the bread of life. He who comes to me will never go hungry, and he who believes in me will never be thirsty" (NIV). That, my friend, is our 24/7 invitation to fully experience the abundant life by continuing to come to the Father through Christ.

The apostle Paul said it this way: "If, when we were God's enemies, we were reconciled to him through the death of his Son, how much more, having been reconciled, shall we be saved through his life!" (Romans 5:10, NIV). In other words, now that we're on God's good side through the grace of Jesus, let's get busy exploring what it means to be alive in Him, what it looks like to treasure Him with all our hearts!

THE MEASURE OF OUR TREASURE

More than a decade ago, I created All Things Southern. It's a website, radio show, and all-around platform where I can be found celebrating the charm and heritage of the South. I chose the egret as my official mascot. I so enjoy watching the long-legged birds stalking our Louisiana lakes that it just seemed fitting to bring them into the family biz. I've since amassed quite a collection of egret pictures and accessories. I have big egrets, little egrets, a metal egret, a porcelain egret, and a fascinating three-foot, artfully carved egret I bought for too much money on a book tour because it called my name! (At least that's what I told The Husband.)

I have a number of other collections that, just between us, aren't nearly as special. Some materialized after I inadvertently mentioned in passing that I liked this or that. See, I made those casual admissions too close to Christmas, and in my big southern family, where everyone is always on the lookout for gift ideas, that kind of thing will buy you a collection every single time! Before you decide I'm an ungrateful soul, let me be quick to assure you that I'm happy to keep these other collections because I appreciate the love behind the purchases. But I keep my egrets because they're special. They're valuable to me because I chose to collect them. Each one holds a memory of where I was or what I was doing when I acquired it, meaning they each have a story that I have *chosen to remember.*

My friend, as surely as I can choose what to collect and value in my home, you and I can choose what we collect and value in our hearts. Choosing All Things Jesus—this is the choice we benefit from making today and tomorrow and the day after that and every day that follows. God's Word repeatedly instructs us to remember God, His name, His words, and His acts.

In Deuteronomy 4:9, Moses said, "Only take heed to yourself, and diligently keep yourself, lest you forget the things your eyes have seen, and lest they depart from your heart all the days of your life. And teach them to your children and your grandchildren" (NKJV).

And again, in Deuteronomy 5:15, God tells the people of Israel to "remember that you were slaves" (NIV). He says the same to those of us on the New Testament side of the Cross. In Ephesians 2:11–12, Paul encouraged believers to remember where God had brought them from and what He had brought them into:

> Therefore remember that formerly you, the Gentiles in the flesh, who are called "Uncircumcision" by the so-called "Circumcision," which is performed in the flesh by human hands—remember that you were at that time separate from Christ, excluded from the commonwealth of Israel, and strangers to the covenants of promise, having no hope and without God in the world.

Oh yes, God wants us to remember Him! One definition of the word *remember* is "to recollect." It means to collect again by remembering. That's exactly my point about choosing our treasure. The things we hear about God can be like a forced collection of knickknacks from family and friends. They won't mean that much unless and until we purposefully hold them in our hearts because we want to store up everything we can learn about Him.

While head knowledge ends up on the shelf gathering dust, real treasure comes from chosen memories of precious firsthand experiences with God. Want even more good news? If we choose to remember Him and collect everything we can discover about Him, God is willing and eager to contribute to our collection on a regular basis as we ask Him to help us value and love Him more. But we'd better be ready to rumble because this is a prayer He loves to answer! It'll also become a prayer you love to pray.

As for your holy collection, it's impossible to spend too much time searching out the mysteries of God's love for us. We can't exhaust the subject because it has no limits. In the third chapter of Ephesians we find these words from Paul:

> For this reason I bow my knees before the Father, from whom every
> family in heaven and on earth derives its name, that He would grant
> you, according to the riches of His glory, to be strengthened with
> power through His Spirit in the inner man, so that Christ may dwell
> in your hearts through faith; and that you, being rooted and
> grounded in love, may be able to comprehend with all the saints what
> is the breadth and length and height and depth, and to know the love
> of Christ which surpasses knowledge, that you may be filled up to all
> the fullness of God.
>
> Now to Him who is able to do far more abundantly beyond all
> that we ask or think, according to the power that works within us, to
> Him be the glory in the church and in Christ Jesus to all generations
> forever and ever. Amen. (verses 14–21)

When we dwell on the breadth, width, length, and height of the love of Jesus, we see it stretching into eternity, and we begin to realize that it's impossible to measure the love of God. But we can have a fine time trying!

Words fail to explain the mystery of God's love and His desire for our company, but the love letter He has written us overflows with this great divine call to friendship, first in the garden and over and over again throughout the Scriptures. Here are just a few examples:

> "Then have them make a sanctuary for me, and I will dwell among
> them." (Exodus 25:8, NIV)

In the beginning was the Word, and the Word was with God, and the Word was God.... The Word became flesh and made his dwelling among us. We have seen his glory, the glory of the One and Only, who came from the Father, full of grace and truth. (John 1:1, 14, NIV)

God, who has called you into fellowship with his Son Jesus Christ our Lord, is faithful. (1 Corinthians 1:9, NIV)

Let's RSVP with a yes to His love and a request that He help us learn to treasure it!

JUST ENOUGH JESUS WILL NEVER BE ENOUGH JESUS

Did I mention that we'll need to make the decision more than once to treasure and respond to God's love? It's vitally important that we learn to repeat this good choice precisely because we so often repeat the wrong ones! We are remedial learners, one and all. If we aren't purposeful about what we choose to value, retain, and treasure, we'll be apt to "taste and see that the LORD is good" (Psalm 34:8) today and look for something else to fill our longing hearts tomorrow.

Oh, for we are clearly born yearning. For more of what, we don't always know, but not knowing what our hearts are longing for doesn't keep us from trying to satisfy them with things, experiences, and people. *More* is our mantra from birth forward, and our constant striving after it never fails to deliver. The problem is, it delivers more dissatisfaction instead of the greater contentment we're anticipating. But what if our insatiable desire for more isn't the problem? *What if this unrelenting hunger is exactly what we've been divinely designed to feel, a gift from God to compel us toward the One our souls really crave?*

Did you know that Ecclesiastes 3:11 tells us that God put *eternity* in our hearts? Consider the implications. It doesn't say we were placed in eternity; it says eternity was placed in us. Forever and a day can be incredibly hard to fathom. Try to think about eternity. Your mind will bail on you every time, the finite staggering before the infinite—and yet God says He placed this open-ended reality in your heart and mine. Amazing! I suspect we haven't begun to scratch the surface of this mysterious gift of eternity, but whatever else it is, I believe it stirs in all of us an inherent awareness of something more, something greater than our current experience, coupled with an insatiable desire to pursue it.

More than a century ago, a well-known English preacher named Charles Spurgeon said, "It is the incessant turmoil of the world, the constant attraction of earthly things which takes away the soul from Christ."[2] It was true then and it's true today. Nothing and no one on this earth can fully satisfy our human hearts. The pursuit of anything and everything temporal will only alienate us from the Creator who sets our hearts to beating, because God Himself is the more we're looking for! He designed us to reach for eternity, found in relationship with Him.

> The very admission that what you're experiencing of God is not enough is setting you up for more.

Perhaps this is why no mortal can adequately explain this life to us. We're dropped somewhere into God's timeline with nothing but the flesh on our bones and a delicious dissatisfaction in our hearts. Even if we should come to faith in Christ, our souls will still die a thousand deaths if we settle for going through the motions of religion. Our restless hearts won't stop longing precisely because there really is more and God wired our hearts to pursue it.

I don't know why you picked up this book. Maybe you've found Jesus to be so sweet you're always on the lookout for more of Him. Maybe you don't honestly want more Jesus but you wish you did. Either way, the very admission that what you're experiencing of Him is not enough is setting you up for more. I liken it to what happens when an extended family gets together and everyone there wants to hold the new baby.

How many times have you seen one relative after another try to soothe the child while the mother looks on, content for a time to let the scene play out? She may watch without intervening while her loved ones try to give the baby a pacifier, change his diaper, or offer him a bottle. One of these efforts may even distract the child for a while. But tell me, what happens when nothing and no one will satisfy that baby but the presence of his dearly beloved mama? You'd better believe it. Score one for baby. He's about to be united with mom.

Likewise, God reserves His intimacy for those unwilling to settle for anything less. If going to church is enough, if being around others who are passionate about Him is enough, if anything short of realizing His intimate presence for ourselves is enough, that's all we'll ever experience.

God knows that His presence is the greatest thrill this world has to offer, that joy and contentment are found in Him, but still He allows us to resist Him. He simply will not drag us kicking and screaming into His presence—even if we do belong to Him.

Some time back I shared with my newspaper readers a family secret my dear husband and I had been living with for way too long. Once, years ago, my husband, Phil, and I forced our early adolescent children onto the biggest roller coaster they'd ever seen—against their will. I know what you're thinking, and you're right. But if I may explain, we callous brutes had our reasons.

For starters, it was late. We were about to leave the famed theme park with its highly publicized ride, and we felt sure we'd never be back. It was now or never. Besides, we knew Jessica and Phillip loved roller coasters. They were just a little intimidated. If we could manage to get 'em on board, we knew they'd thank us later. I'm not excusing us, but somehow the two of us convinced ourselves we were doing the right thing.

As hard as it is to admit, Phil and I each took a child and began to drag, pull, and coax them up the long ramp. The poor babies whimpered and begged while we pleaded. We could feel the reproachful looks being thrown at us by the teenage attendants and the other straggling theme parkers, but we knew our kids would love the ride once we got them on it. For what it's worth, we were right. Several wild, fun-packed, squealing moments later, we pulled back into the roller coaster station with those very same kids begging to go again. But by this time, reason had returned and Phil and I were more sheepish than smug. I feel guilty every time I think of that story. I'm also awed every time, awed that a God big enough to compel us to do anything He wishes would restrain Himself from overriding our free will.

> At the core of my "not having enough Jesus" problem lay all my previous efforts to have "just enough" Jesus!

Indeed, God placed this desire for more in us so that we might search for Him of our own volition. I've taken to calling it a blessed dissatisfaction. God knows that yielding our lives to Him brings us this life's ultimate pleasure, but unlike me and my man, He's not going to force anyone to go along with His plan.

Sometimes I wish God wasn't such a gentleman. The more I taste of His sweet presence, the more I wish He'd grab everyone else by the arm and pull them onto the ride of their lives (or at least let me manhandle 'em, what with my experience and all), but deep down I know that forced companionship isn't friendship.

Remember my flypaper commitment? When I decided I absolutely had to know Jesus now, on this earth, in this lifetime—instead of living in anticipation of seeing Him in the next—I had no way of knowing that commitment would be the catalyst for a completely new life. I didn't realize that looking and listening for Him in His Word would create in me the sweetest of addictions to His friendship. I was simply ready to admit that what I had wasn't enough. I was soon to discover that at the core of my "not having enough Jesus" problem lay all my previous efforts to have "just enough" Jesus. Oh mercy, the rubber is slapping the road now!

THE PROBLEM WITH JUST ENOUGH

If, like me, you want to stay fit but have a hard time squeezing those daily workouts into your tight schedule, I have good news. It turns out that fifteen minutes a day is all you need! Oh yes, according to a recent study, there's no need to run six miles a day or sweat to the oldies for a solid hour with Richard "Spandex" Simmons. Growing evidence suggests that you can cut in half the previously recommended thirty minutes of aerobic activity per day and still reap some nice health benefits.

I was as excited to hear this news as the perky little newscaster seemed to be as she shared it. My first thought was, "Yippy Skippy!" Have I mentioned that I live in the Deep South, otherwise known as the Land of Humidity? Dixie Belle, my beloved but spoiled canine, and I feel as if we're going for a swim every time we venture outdoors for our evening walk. Did I like the idea of cutting that walk in half? You betcha!

Then I found myself musing a little deeper into the idea of "just enough."

It's been my experience that shooting for the minimum requirement in most anything tends to return minimum results. Yet we are all prone to taking that route by default: *How far do I have to walk to get the benefit? What's the lowest grade I can make on this test—and still pass? How many sick days can I take without jeopardizing my job?*

Aiming for the minimum requirement is one thing when it comes to physical exercise and passing grades (worst-case scenario: you'll be a slightly fleshy, average student), but it's a seriously handicapped starting point for anyone who wants to experience an authentic, abundant life in Jesus Christ. *How long is long enough to pray? How much is enough Bible reading? How much am I expected to give, to forgive, to love? When is enough, enough?* Trying to follow Jesus just enough to get to heaven will never satisfy the eternity in our hearts, the yearning for God that is woven into the very fabric of our souls. And it will never, ever fix our broken want-tos! On the other hand I can promise that when our "just enough" turns into "I can't get enough," we find that He is a gracious plenty.

Allow me to explain exactly what this just-enough mentality looked like earlier in my life. Have you ever heard someone described as being so heavenly minded that she's no earthly good? Believe me when I tell you that there was no danger of my falling into that category. Nada, zilch, no way.

In the years before my low burn turned into a boil, I was trying to follow Christ "just enough"—just enough to stay on His good side, just enough to avoid His wrath, just enough to secure me one of those mansions in glory. As long as I checked off my church attendance and daily devotion, I considered myself free and paid up, so to speak, until the next time. My life in between church and daily devotions I saw as precisely that: *my* life.

My mentality had nothing to do with wanting to stray from the church's teachings and everything to do with buying into the Enemy's twisted but effective deception: I was sure that if I cashed everything in for Christ, my life would be bland and boring. I could not have been more wrong. When I finally stepped out of my "just enough" mind-set, I discovered that an all-out pursuit of Jesus Christ equals a hold-on-to-your-hat adventure!

It's as if He says, "So, you say you're ready to go with Me? Well, darling, let's dance!" Oh, and have we ever danced! We've danced the slow songs while tears ran down my cheeks, and we've shaken a leg on the fast ones as my heart soared. I admit with great regret that I have even sat out a few dances in a huff. But once I decided I absolutely had to know Him, once I gave up my average Christian life for the unknown and put my shaky hand in His, God began to transform my dry, checklist living, and He has never stopped. He joins me in the Scriptures, and He meets me in prayer when I come, not looking to feel good about myself, but longing to know more about Him. He has shown me the secret of abiding in His love by choosing His ways over my own, and He has opened my eyes to the beauty of His body, the church.

We'll talk more in the coming pages about giving up the status quo, what that has looked like in my life, and how He has met me in the search. Right now I want to be clear that it's not just me or your pastor or some third-world missionary who has access to this abundant life in Christ. Father God loves you with a steadfast love. He wants to do life with you. You're not an isolated case, someone who can't find God. He is just as available to you as He has been to any other human being who has ever drawn a breath. This is His promise: "You will seek Me and find Me when you search for Me with all your heart" (Jeremiah 29:13).

Dear one, get thyself into the hunt!

Dear Lord, I don't want just enough Jesus to get to heaven. I want more! Give me the desire to love You

23

with all my heart, soul, and mind. Help me know the width, depth, length, and height of Christ's love for me. Lead me into the adventure of divine friendship with You. Open my heart wide to understand and experience Your love for me and to increasingly love You more in return. Amen.

2

COURAGE FOR US
NOT-SO-SUPER SAINTS

"Lord, I want to abandon everything to follow You, but I'm scared of what that might look like!"

One morning while simultaneously blow-drying my hair, doing leg lunges on my Total Gym, and channel-surfing the tube, I paused on a Christian broadcast. (Yes, I was multitasking long before they gave it a name.) Although I'd missed most of the program, I was delighted to find one of my favorite recording artists closing the show with the incredibly beautiful worship song "One Desire." Within moments the divinely inspired lyrics filling the room moved me to stop everything and simply soak in His sweet presence.

I wasn't the only one who heard the call to worship that morning. The camera paused several times on a lady in the audience who was visibly as touched as I was. Her head was slightly bowed but not so much that you couldn't see the emotion gripping her heart. As the last notes began to fade, I saw this lady make a move to rise to her feet in what I can only imagine was going to be a heartfelt ovation for the singer or a spontaneous act of praise to God. We'll never know. Just as quickly as she began to rise, she noticed that no one else was moving, and she froze in her seat, too intimidated to follow through with the impulse.

Oh, do understand—I'm not judging this dear worshiper. I was in the comfort of my own bedroom, remember? She was sitting in the middle of a studio audience. Besides, even if I haven't done that very same thing, I've surely made similar choices. I'm not proud of it, but at times I've held back in the enthusiastic expression of my own faith because of what I believed people around me were doing or thinking.

For example, I've dialed down the passion for All Things Jesus in my conversation when I'm around people who aren't craving more of Him, compared to how freely I speak around those who are. I've placated my conscience with the lame defense that I don't want to offend people, but that's not entirely true. Sometimes I'd rather blend in because standing out makes me feel different, exposed, vulnerable.

The sort of intimidation I've just described remains an unfamiliar foe as long as we settle for going back and forth to church and simply professing faith in a God we don't really know. We won't feel a burning desire to speak of One whose name doesn't light a spark in our own hearts. But this internal conflict quickly becomes an issue for anyone willing to pray as we did in chapter 1. Anyone who decides there has to be more to following Jesus than she is experiencing and professes her desire to find it, anyone who admits that she doesn't love God like she should and asks Him to help her love Him more, will most surely encounter a sneaky opponent in the form of intimidation.

Learning to recognize intimidation is crucial, for much like the worshiper in that studio audience, succumbing to it keeps us from living with our hearts wide open to His Spirit. Every single time we try to weigh what other people may think of us against our desire for more of God, we risk settling for what we've experienced in Him instead of reaching for the richer life He offers.

Intimidation says the status quo Christian life is enough and chides us for wanting more. (Aren't you taking this Jesus thing too far?) Intimidation encourages us to please others instead of living for God, and it pressures us to accept the conclusions others have drawn from their own religious experiences instead of seeking His truth for ourselves. Intimidation may present itself as the fear of looking foolish or the fear of failure, and it often hounds us with the suggestion that we don't measure up and we never will. Regardless of the form it takes, this much we can be sure of: left unchecked, intimidation robs us of our God dreams.

One Christmas season years ago, I took my then four-year-old daughter to *The Nutcracker.* The stage lights bounced off the glow in Jessica's eyes as we whispered together about her own dance lessons being right around the corner! I had signed her up for classes that coming spring, and my little girl found the idea all consuming.

Excitement reached a fever pitch by the time that first class rolled around. I helped Jessica wiggle into thick pink tights and a shiny black leotard, slipped on her pink tulle skirt and ballet slippers, and tied a pink ribbon around her long blond ponytail. I still treasure the picture of her posing proudly at the front door of our home with that matching pink ballerina duffle bag on her shoulder, totally oblivious to the charming hint of leftover baby belly swelling her midsection. Oh, yes! She was a ballerina in the making, at least in the comfort zone of her familiar surroundings.

A short drive later, the two of us arrived at the First United Methodist Church, where classes were to be held in the fellowship hall. We took a seat to wait our turn, and Jessica Ann chattered nonstop—until the other dancers started to arrive. The more the waiting area filled, the closer Jessica pressed in to my side. By the time the double doors opened and her teacher stepped out, my prima ballerina's confidence had melted into her tiny slippers. She attached herself to my legs and began whispering, then outright begging for me to take her home. Miss Missy, the dance teacher, had a regal bearing, gained, I would imagine, from her own years of dance training. Dressed in her own dance attire, she must have looked to Jessica like she'd stepped straight out of *The Nutcracker*. It took a lot of enticing from Miss Missy and whispered promises from me to get Jessica through those big double doors.

Jessica pressed through her fears to stick out that first year of dance lessons and many more until she finally decided to pursue other interests, but she never lost her admiration for Miss Missy. From the first lesson to the last, Jessica held her teacher in the highest regard. I'll always remember the season-ending recital when Jessica sat with her little friends after their own well-rehearsed numbers and watched their revered dance teacher performing the finale. As Miss Missy twirled and spun about in a beautiful flowing costume to the soundtrack of "Wind Beneath My Wings," we parents watched the shining and awestruck eyes of her young students follow her every move. By the time the music faded and the lyrics asked for the last time, "Did you ever know that you're my hero?" one thing was clear to everyone present. As far as our daughters were concerned, Miss Missy was precisely that.

SUPERHEROES CAN BE OVERRATED

Role models are good. Spiritual role models are invaluable. It's superheroes that can be overrated! And yet, as believers, we have a tendency to make superheroes out of other Christians by deciding that they have obtained a measure of maturity that is beyond our reach. Granted, some people may aspire to that kind of role, but most of the time our superheroes in the faith are drafted into this tenuous position. The wise ones don't want the title, and for good reason.

Superhero Christianity is dangerous for all involved. It can set the superheroes up for a fall, and it can encourage overawed fans to camp in the audience instead of pressing on toward the greater goal of knowing God for themselves.

Miss Missy's finale was never intended to intimidate her class; it was meant to inspire them to reach for their own dancing dreams. The obvious passion of other believers offers each of us a similar choice. When we watch a friend leave behind a comfortable life to move to Rwanda and make her home among strangers in order to share God's love, or when our neighbor faces down cancer with grace and a smile, or when we meet someone whose love for Jesus seems bigger than life, we can declare ourselves too inadequate for such a passionate pursuit of Christ— or we can let their examples inspire us to run that much harder after Him ourselves!

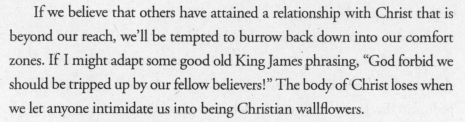

We are entitled to an above-average life in Christ not because *we* want it but because He does!

If we believe that others have attained a relationship with Christ that is beyond our reach, we'll be tempted to burrow back down into our comfort zones. If I might adapt some good old King James phrasing, "God forbid we should be tripped up by our fellow believers!" The body of Christ loses when we let anyone intimidate us into being Christian wallflowers.

The astounding good news of the gospel is that all of God is available to all of us through Jesus, Immanuel, *God with us.* When we're tempted to think we're not capable or deserving of a richer, deeper faith, it helps to remember that we are entitled to an above-average life in Christ not simply because *we* want it but because He does. Jesus said, "The thief comes only in order to steal and kill and destroy. I came that they may have and enjoy life, and have it in abundance (to the full, till it overflows)" (John 10:10, AMP).

Jesus lived a perfect life and offered it up for us on the cross. He tasted death, triumphed over the grave, and returned to heaven, all to give you and me access to His Father and ours, to give us life that overflows. Oh, my friend, if only we could grasp the truth that God isn't just tolerating us. He doesn't welcome those superheroes we deem more worthy any differently than He welcomes us. Jesus's mission is fulfilled. We are each fully accepted, and we can all experience what it means to live life in Him—unless we allow ourselves to be intimidated by other people or mired in our own sense of failure or inferiority.

You wouldn't know it by visiting with her today, but there was a time when my middle sister was easily intimidated. During our growing up years, Rhonda—the one our family and friends nicknamed Pretty Woman—didn't like to go anywhere unless I went with her. If we happened to go some-place separately, Rhonda would beg me to wait for her at the door if I arrived first. That way she could go in with me—only she meant behind me. Yours truly, the youngest of the three sisters, entered every room with Rhonda walking so closely behind me that we were likely to fall like dominoes if I stopped too quickly.

It didn't make sense. Rhonda had long blond hair and pretty blue eyes, the type of looks people are naturally inclined to respond to positively. I, on the other hand, was the brunette with the hoot-owl glasses and a speech impediment that lasted well into my adolescent years. But it was useless to point these things out to Rhonda. She simply didn't feel confident going in alone.

It's beyond sad to think of how many people spend their lives dependent on others for a taste of God, much like Rhonda depended on me for moral support all those years ago. "Pray for me," they'll say, attaching little worth to their own efforts at reaching the throne. "I'm not as strong as you are," they'll say to their pastor, teacher, or friend. "I don't have your kind of faith."

Please understand. There's nothing wrong with a prayer request. The Bible encourages us to pray for one another. We have nothing to lose and much to gain in asking for prayer. But you and I forfeit our own great blessing of doing life with God if we think others have His ear and we don't!

Unrestricted access to God's throne, secured through the blood of Jesus, is available to anyone willing to bend her knee before Him. We're welcomed through the favor of His beloved Son. The opportunity isn't secured through any merit of our own but is freely given to all who believe. It's as if Jesus calls from His seat at the Father's right hand, "You woke up worthy; I'll meet you at the door." Or, as He says in John 10:9, "I am the door; if anyone enters through Me, he will be saved, and will go in and out and find pasture."

According to Romans 12:3, "God has allotted to each a measure of faith." The question isn't "What's wrong with my measure?" but "What will I do with my measure?"

GIVING UP STATUS QUO FOR GUNG-HO!

No one gets a head start on this great faith adventure. Regardless of our back-stories, all believers begin at the same place with God: hopeless, sinful, and separated from Him forever until we come seeking forgiveness, then fully reconciled and set on our way once we accept the atoning blood of Jesus. In other words, the road to *The Nutcracker* runs straight through the "Bunny Hop." The ballerina who gets the leading role in *Swan Lake* was once a beginner learning her basic positions.

> We are mirrors whose brightness, if we are bright, is
> wholly derived from the sun that shines upon us.
> —C. S. Lewis, *The Four Loves*

Though we all start from the same place of utter dependence on God for our purpose and worth, our experience pursuing Him won't be exactly like anyone else's. Our God is all about individuality. Your faith walk will be as unique as you are. (I dare you not to think about a snowflake right now.)

I remember when my oldest sister's daughter unwittingly put on an adorable display of individuality during her own early dance years. If my Jessica came to the stage with a bit of hesitation, Hillary took to it as if it were her birthright. That year Hillary's class of budding dancers had practiced and polished a rousing number set to the tune of "Come Up and See Me Sometime." They wore rocking red outfits, and Hillary "boop-oop-ee-dooped" with the best of 'em. As the music ended, each little ballerina was to leave her place in line, approach center stage, and curtsy to the audience before exiting stage left. When her turn came, my overly eager little niece took center stage with gusto, but in her excitement she accidentally turned around and bowed booty first—showcasing her matching red bloomers for the crowd. It's no exaggeration to say that Hillary brought down the house. As the audience clapped and roared with laughter, Hillary scampered off feeling quite pleased with the response and totally oblivious to the blooper that elicited it.

Based on His own Word, I can assure you that Father God finds your individuality as charming as we found Hillary's! Psalm 139 is a passage worth feasting on anytime you need to shore up your shaky self-confidence about your place in God's heart. In a chapter replete with assurances that God formed you and knew you in your mother's womb and that He is intimately acquainted with all His kids, we find these words: "How precious also are Your thoughts to me, O God! How vast is the sum of them! If I should count them, they would outnumber the sand. When I awake, I am still with You" (verses 17–18). God didn't base His design on an earlier model during His skillful weaving of you in your mother's womb. He made you *you,* and He is inviting you to lose yourself to find a bigger life in Him.

I'm beside myself with excitement about getting into the Scriptures with you to look at God's superpowerful provision for conquering intimidation of any stripe, but first, let's expose one more form that might be the most prevalent. As intimidated as we may be by other people or by our own insecurities, we often find ourselves much more intimidated by the idea of letting God be God of our entire lives. It scares us to consider the consequences of allowing God to reach beyond the faith corner we've carefully arranged for Him. We want to experience His presence, and we want to see Him move around us—as long as He doesn't move in us or on us in a way that we find uncomfortable or, worse yet, undignified.

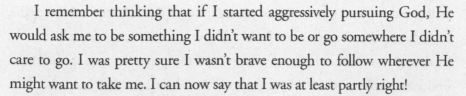

Remember, the Author of our
faith isn't finished with it.

I remember thinking that if I started aggressively pursuing God, He would ask me to be something I didn't want to be or go somewhere I didn't care to go. I was pretty sure I wasn't brave enough to follow wherever He might want to take me. I can now say that I was at least partly right!

What I didn't understand was that none of us can find the courage in our own cowardly hearts to pursue this God Man wherever He leads. However—and this is an incredibly delicious and powerful *however*—the sweet promise of His Word is that the courage we need is readily available. Remember, the Author of our faith isn't finished with it. Everything we need to go further, deeper, and higher is already ours.

We need not be one bit brave to live the accepted, expected, unremarkable Christian life, but we will need courage to relax our hold on everything familiar and ask Him to show up in our lives without setting conditions for what that will look like. As believers, this kind of courage is our inheritance! In one of His last conversations with His most intimate friends, Jesus told them not to be afraid, to follow Him courageously—but He did so only after explaining that He would equip them (and us!) for just such a full-throttle ride.

CHRIST, THE REWARD OF THE RISKY

The scene we want to explore opens in the book of John where Jesus and His disciples have just finished celebrating the Passover meal. We often refer to this event as the Last Supper, but at the time, Jesus was the only one there who knew they were breaking bread together for the final time before His crucifixion. His men were still confused. Though they had just witnessed a sober exchange between Jesus and Judas, they were unable to understand the devastating seriousness of the Lord's words when He told His betrayer, "What you are about to do, do quickly" (John 13:27, NIV). However, once Judas Iscariot left the room, Jesus looked around the table at His closest friends and began a farewell speech with an unmistakable message: the time had come for Him to die.

This wasn't the first time Jesus told the disciples why He had come to earth and how it would all end, but up until this point the message had been understandably hard for His friends to hear. Matthew and Mark both recorded Peter's impulsive reaction to one such troubling announcement from their beloved leader:

> From that time on Jesus began to explain to his disciples that he must
> go to Jerusalem and suffer many things at the hands of the elders,
> chief priests and teachers of the law, and that he must be killed and on
> the third day be raised to life. Peter took him aside and began to
> rebuke him. "Never, Lord!" he said. "This shall never happen to you!"
> (Matthew 16:21–22, NIV)

They also recorded Jesus's forceful response:

> Jesus turned and said to Peter, "Get behind me, Satan! You are a
> stumbling block to me; you do not have in mind the things of God,
> but the things of men." (verse 23, NIV)

Ouch! Perhaps the men made a conscious decision not to think about what Jesus said would happen in Jerusalem after that strong rebuke! Or maybe they did try to figure out what this suffering and dying was about but gave up in confusion. Either way, the gospel accounts make it obvious that the boys continued to find it difficult to reconcile Jesus's often-repeated death announcements with their dreams of His prophesied kingdom.

Mark recounted one such conversation among the disciples on the heels of a statement Jesus made about His impending death. The way Jesus called them out on it might be comical if it weren't so serious.

> They left that place and passed through Galilee. Jesus did not want anyone to know where they were, because he was teaching his disciples. He said to them, "The Son of Man is going to be betrayed into the hands of men. They will kill him, and after three days he will rise." But they did not understand what he meant and were afraid to ask him about it.
>
> They came to Capernaum. When he was in the house, he asked them, "What were you arguing about on the road?" But they kept quiet because on the way they had argued about who was the greatest. (Mark 9:30–34, NIV)

(I think I would've kept quiet too!)

But now we find the little band gathered in the upper room for Passover. And this time when Jesus announced that the purpose for which He came had arrived and He would be leaving them, He made a distinction from all those earlier pronouncements—a distinction that blasted through their misconceptions and morphed their confusion into full-blown anxiety.

"Little children," Jesus said with tender affection. "I am with you a little while longer. You will seek Me; and as I said to the Jews, now I also say to you, 'Where I am going, you cannot come'" (John 13:33).

With those words, the men finally understood that their time with Jesus was drawing to a close. Their brave, wise, miracle-working leader was going away, and they wouldn't be able to follow Him.

Aware that this news rocked their world, Jesus moved to comfort them. In the opening verses of the next chapter, He began an incredibly rich discourse to strengthen their wobbly knees. His words can slay the intimidation in our hearts too, if we'll let them.

> Do not let your heart be troubled; believe in God, believe also in Me.
> In My Father's house are many dwelling places; if it were not so, I
> would have told you; for I go to prepare a place for you. If I go and
> prepare a place for you, I will come again and receive you to Myself,
> that where I am, there you may be also. (John 14:1–3)

I liken this scene and Jesus's encouraging words to what happens when it comes time to say good-bye to my grandchildren. My grandchildren all call me Keggie, and it has nothing to do with a keg. It's a throwback to the days when my nieces and nephews tried to say Aunt Shellie. The closest thing they could come up with was Aunt Keggie, and it stuck. Years later when the grandchildren started coming, people told me that once the kids began talking they would probably give me another name of their own choosing, but no, they surprised us and stayed with Keggie.

Hearing a sweet little trembling voice say, "Do you have to go, Keggie?" is enough to melt me on the spot. I often console them by pointing out something we have planned for the future. "You're coming to see me next week," I'll say before going on to describe the various things I have planned for us to do together. All of my efforts, all of my encouraging words are designed to see the storm clouds roll away from their little faces. This is the kind of tenderness I see from Jesus recorded in John 14, and it never fails to move me.

I find it fascinating that one of the first things Jesus said to calm the anxious hearts of His men was, "Believe in God, believe also in Me." It's worth emphasizing who Jesus was trying to buck up here. He wasn't talking to a crowd of unbelievers, to the doubting and jeering multitudes; He was addressing His right-hand men! Jesus was trying to still the trembling knees of His most intimate friends and "bestest" buddies who had just heard Him predict some serious developments! These men had left everything to follow Jesus, yet here in this most intimate moment, He told them to "believe in Me."

Whatever should we make of this tender instruction? Didn't the disciples already believe in Jesus? Yes, of course they did. Jesus was speaking a gentle reminder to their quaking hearts. Oh, that we would let it soothe our fearful ones too. He was asking them to take their faith in "God out there" and find peace in knowing the "God right here."

Jesus encouraged His knee-knocking men to step out on everything He had been teaching them. He urged them—if they believed in God, and if they believed He was the Son of God—to also believe that His death would be a new beginning and not a tragic ending. In the subsequent verses, Jesus expounded on this promise, pledging to His friends that His supreme sacrifice at the cross would fling open the door to the Father and make it possible for everyone who believes to walk and talk with Him, right here on earth.

> Jesus asks us to take our faith in "God out there" and find peace in knowing the "God right here."

I know God can seem far away, cold, and distant to us. But far more important, *Jesus* knows it. Believing in God way up there doesn't comfort our troubled hearts. Believing that, out of His great love for us, He sent His only begotten Son to redeem us, to live smack in the middle of this hard and broken world with us, and then to lead us home—this comforts, and it gives our timid hearts a boost of divine courage.

Jesus is the exact representation of our invisible God. Consider how the author of Hebrews described Him:

Who being the brightness of His glory and the express image of His
person, and upholding all things by the word of His power, when He
had by Himself purged our sins, sat down at the right hand of the
Majesty on high, having become so much better than the angels, as
He has by inheritance obtained a more excellent name than they.
(1:3–4, NKJV)

Eternal life has already begun for those of us who believe in Jesus. He isn't just the door to heaven at the end of our journey on earth; He is the door to enjoying our journey on earth, to knowing God and living daily with Him.

As the men were absorbing their leader's assurance that the antidote for their fears was to fasten their courage in all that He had promised them as the Son of God, Jesus made a seemingly incredible statement: "You know the way where I am going" (John 14:4).

Apparently this was too much for Thomas, who dared to register his instant objection. Allow me the liberty of adding some emphasis, for this is the way I hear the disciple's complaint: "Thomas said to Him, 'Lord, we do not know *where* You are going, how do we know *the way*?'" (verse 5).

> This wild and untamed Jesus will ruin you
> for anything this world has to offer!

History has recorded this disciple as Doubting Thomas, but he sounds more like Honest Thomas in this passage. I liken his gut response to how discomfiting it feels when we wish we were bold enough to follow Jesus wherever He might lead, but we don't know where to start. Worse still, we can't seem to loosen our iron grasp on what we think we want out of this life long enough to discover the one He has planned for us. We want Him to conform to our limited ideas of who He is because we're scared of letting Him be I AM. Afraid to explore the siren call of Jesus Christ for fear of where He might take us, we choose the default option of attending church to please Him and living our lives to please us.

The reality is that God rarely reveals the details of where He is going and what He is doing. He simply discloses the intimacies of His own glorious nature to the one who seeks Him, and these glimpses of glory will make the most cowardly lion lose interest in the itinerary and chase after the shining light of His presence. This wild and untamed Jesus we're after is both alluring and potentially dangerous. He will ruin you for anything else this world has to offer. However, it is a sweet "ruination," because the weaker the hold temporal things have on us, the freer we are to lose ourselves in the One who placed eternity in our hearts.

THE GREAT UNKNOWN

Sometimes what Jesus doesn't say is as intriguing as what He does. Why didn't Jesus tell the disciples, "You know where I'm going"? Wouldn't that have been more helpful? Instead, He told the men they knew *the way* where He was going.

I don't pretend to have the definitive explanation of this curious statement, but I will tell you what it says to me: When Jesus speaks of my final destination in heaven, I'm relieved. When He assures me that I know the way there, my courage gets a booster shot! The Son of God walked this earth as Son of Man. He understood that His men were scared to go on without Him, and He knows more fully than we ever could that you and I desperately need a "today Jesus." Watch as He responds with incredible patience.

In answer to Thomas's question, "How do we know the way?" Jesus said, "I am the way, and the truth, and the life; no one comes to the Father but through Me. If you had known Me, you would have known My Father also; from now on you know Him, and have seen Him" (John 14:6–7).

With that, Philip took his turn to complain. Jesus said the disciples had seen God, but Philip didn't think so. He proposed a deal. Philip said, "Lord, show us the Father and that will be enough for us" (John 14:8, NIV).

I understand these men. In the coming chapters, I'll tell you more about my own deal-making days with the Father as I begged Him to show up and make the lights blink or the curtains move—anything to let me know He was there. Like Thomas and Philip and the rest of the disciples, I've been convinced that I didn't know the way to live this God life. I suspect you have too, but Jesus says we do know. Don't you love that?

Finding our way from warming a church pew to an all-out pursuit of this great God of ours is an ongoing adventure. I cannot emphasize enough that this isn't about signing up for a spiritual self-improvement course. It's about falling in love with Jesus, one faltering step at a time. It comforts me to hear Jesus tell the disciples they know the way, even if His men weren't so sure.

In the next verses, Jesus gently rebuked Philip for not understanding that they had already seen God. He encouraged all the men to believe His words when He declared that He and the Father are one, adding that even if they couldn't believe His words, they should believe the works they had seen Him perform. Either way, Jesus knew that His men were equipped to walk by faith, and He knows we are too. Read with me how He spelled out in spine-strengthening prose exactly why we can walk in this same confident assurance.

If you love me, you will obey what I command. And I will ask the Father, and he will give you another Counselor to be with you forever—the Spirit of truth. The world cannot accept him, because it neither sees him nor knows him. But you know him, for he lives with you and will be in you. I will not leave you as orphans; I will come to you. Before long, the world will not see me anymore, but you will see me. Because I live, you also will live. On that day you will realize that I am in my Father, and you are in me, and I am in you. Whoever has my commands and obeys them, he is the one who loves me. He who loves me will be loved by my Father, and I too will love him and show myself to him." (John 14:15–21, NIV)

Jesus's reassuring message to His weak-in-the-knees men was that He would be as near to them as He had ever been because He would soon live in them through the gift of the Holy Spirit. I'm tempted to go all caps and smiley faces. This, my friend, is how you and I can find the courage, strength, and hope to follow wherever He leads—by learning to draw on the limitless resources of the all-powerful God whose Spirit dwells in us, right here, right now.

Jesus made a way for the Spirit of God to live in us while we are still living in this world. This unprecedented access to God knows no bounds because He doesn't. Incredible, isn't it? If we read on, we'll see that at least one of the men who heard those words in real time thought it sounded too good to be true.

Then Judas (not Judas Iscariot) said, "But, Lord, why do you intend to show yourself to us and not to the world?"

Jesus replied, "If anyone loves me, he will obey my teaching. My Father will love him, and we will come to him and make our home with him." (John 14:22–23, NIV)

That's not a "some fine day on the other side of the rainbow" promise, dear friend. That's for the here and now on planet Earth! Jesus promised His friends that His coming death and resurrection would set the stage for them to walk and talk with Him and His Father through the Holy Spirit.

Jesus left to prepare a place for us, to make a way for us to be with Him and His Father, *beginning now*. As surely as He left, Jesus will come again one glorious day to take us to heaven, but—oh, drink in the glorious news—to those who believe, He comes in the power of the Holy Spirit to live in us now, on this side of eternity, and lead us home! As the apostle Paul explained, "Now it is God who makes both us and you stand firm in Christ. He anointed us, set his seal of ownership on us, and put his Spirit in our hearts as a deposit, guaranteeing what is to come" (2 Corinthians 1:21–22, NIV).

This was Jesus's good news to the disciples, and it is our bank-it courage: you're not on this great adventure by your lonesome little self, and neither am I! (Seriously, I may need someone to shout with me.) This is the special heritage of those who trust in Jesus. That acceleration in your pulse? That would be your courage rising. Run with it.

Take a Deep Breath and Jump with Jesus

Back in my daughter's "Bunny Hop" recital days, Miss Missy would stand below the stage and dance along with her littlest students during their numbers so they could mimic her movements. Even if they knew the routine, her presence inspired them with confidence when the lights lowered. The only thing better would have been for her to be in their heads, directing them every step of the way. Such inside-out leading is exactly what we enjoy through the Spirit of Grace that lives in us.

We don't have to be afraid of falling if we're leaning on the One who never fails!

Over and over in the Gospels, Jesus told people to "take courage."[3] Today He says the same to you and me. Courage is readily available to Christ's followers because courage lives in us through the Holy Spirit. Could you use more courage to follow Christ? It is yours for the asking. Reach out to Him! As long as we are walking in the Light, there's always more.

Among the assurances Jesus gave His followers as He prepared to leave them was this mind-boggling promise: "In that day you will ask in My name, and I do not say to you that I will request of the Father on your behalf; for the Father Himself loves you, because you have loved Me and have believed that I came forth from the Father" (John 16:26–27).

Now there's a truckload of courage for all comers! Your belief in Jesus qualifies you as one of God's favorites. Okay, maybe I'm paraphrasing, but here's the bottom line: Jesus said the Father has a special love for *you* because of your belief in His Son.

Too cool! Finally, we can all be the Teacher's pet! (Back in the day, I always envied the kid who got to be the teacher's pet. For some reason nonstop talkers like me seldom enjoyed that distinction. I don't understand it either. I was just trying to keep things moving.)

My friend, are you a believer? Then revel in God's love for you because of your belief in Jesus. Your secure role as Teacher's pet is all the more reason not to be intimidated—not by a spiritual giant, a superhero, or your own weakness. Try whistling that tune the next time you feel intimidation stalking on all sides.

**Your love for Jesus endears you
to His Father and ours!**

Courage to begin following Jesus and courage to continue are both found by training our eyes on Him. To be unwilling to risk moving toward the promises of God is to forfeit them. Whereas it takes little courage to give ourselves to the outward facade of Christianity, it requires the fortitude of constant surrender to yield ourselves to His leading. But if we want an uncommon life in Christ, we'll need to take a deep breath and choose the uncommon way.

I was eight or nine years old the first time I remember someone telling me to take a deep breath. My oldest sister, Cyndie, was encouraging me to bail off the top of Papa's pump shed. "You can do it, Shellie. Just take a deep breath and jump!" From where I sat, crouched at the edge of the roof, it looked like an awful long way to the grass, but Cyndie had just performed the miraculous feat before my very eyes, and she looked none the worse for wear. I looked at Rhonda, who stood quietly beside Cyndie. Our middle sister shrugged as if to say, "It's your call." I caught my breath and jumped.

At some point or another, we've all been told to take a deep physical breath. It's meant to be calming, relaxing, even energizing. And it is, up to a point. But I'm suggesting a fortifying breath of another sort, one that is immeasurably superior. If going deeper with God feels like the biggest pumpshed jump of your life, remember that help is only a whispered prayer away. Steady yourself in His love, be encouraged by the promises found in His Word, take a deep breath—and jump! And then jump again tomorrow, and the day after that.

Before we leave intimidation in our trail dust, I must offer one last warning: Sometimes intimidation masquerades as realism. It sounds like this: "*Most* people don't take the Bible *that* seriously. You need to be realistic."

Oh, dear one, has the admonition to "be realistic" ever caused your heart to beat faster? That's what I thought. We need to run in the opposite direction of anyone who tells us to be realistic. Instead, let's listen to the One who describes Himself in Jeremiah: "Thus says the LORD who made the earth, the LORD who formed it to establish it, the LORD is His name" (33:2).

Let's respond with hearts wide open to His soul-stirring invitation that follows that divine introduction: "Call to Me and I will answer you, and I will tell you great and mighty things, which you do not know" (verse 3).

Lord, I don't want to live a status quo Christian life. Give me the courage to break free of everything that intimidates me, even the good examples of other believers, and to live the life You came to give me. According to Your Word, we've all been given a measure of faith to believe. Help me use that measure to start where I am today and begin to live fearlessly in my faith. Give me courage to risk my average life to gain the abundant one promised me in Christ Jesus. Amen.

I SUPPOSE CLIFFSNOTES ARE OUT

*"Lord, they say I can come to know
You through Your Word, but I don't like
to read the Bible! Help me develop
a love for Your truth!"*

The house was still. It was just me and Connor Phillip Maher, my newest grandson. I had convinced Connor's mommy to let me have the midnight feeding so she could get some much-needed rest. Behind our rocker, the moon flooded in through the window and over my shoulder, bathing the room in a soft glow that was just bright enough to illuminate the tiny features of my newest love. A trickle of milk escaped perfect little lips, and I smiled.

My grandson was in what I fondly call "the milk coma," that seemingly unconscious state that befalls a newborn with a full belly, but I knew that in three short hours—give or take a second—Connor would be gnawing at the burp cloth as I hurried to tuck it under his chin. And those itty-bitty fingers, the ones that had only just now relaxed their grip on mine, they'd be clutching frantically for the next meal. It's baby language for *I want more and I don't mean maybe.*

The apostle Peter used this picture of desperate dependency to lay out the believer's growth plan.

Therefore, putting aside all malice and all deceit and hypocrisy and envy and all slander, like newborn babies, long for the pure milk of the word, so that by it you may grow in respect to salvation, if you have tasted the kindness of the Lord.
(1 Peter 2:1–3)

The image of longing "for the pure milk of the word" speaks as clearly to us today as it must have to the first generation of Christ followers. If we're going to let the God who made this world light up our own—if we're going to move beyond mundane faith to the joy of endless discovery with Him—a healthy respect for God's Word won't be enough, girlfriend. We'll need to live on it.

> We won't begin to know the life we were born to live without feeding on eternal truth.

Jesus wasn't reciting Deuteronomy 8:3 just for kicks when He said, "Man does not live on bread alone, but on every word that comes from the mouth of God" (Matthew 4:4, NIV). He was planting His own life on His Father's powerful revelation: We might exist through physical nourishment. We might breathe in and we might breathe out, but we won't begin to know the life we were born to live without feeding on eternal truth.

While I've become addicted to reading God's Word and hearing Him talk to me through it, I need you to know that this has not always been the case. There was a time when I carried around an ever-present load of guilt about my experience with the Good Book. Are you ready for my deep, dark secret? For the life of me, I could not quit drooling on its holy pages! I'm not talking about salivating over the tasty bread of heaven. This was the shame of any aspiring Bible student: sleep slobber.

STUMBLING IN FAMILIAR CIRCLES

I wanted my early morning Bible sessions to be inspirational, instructive, and life changing. They were boring, bland, and guilt inducing. Looking back, I can see a number of reasons for the chasm between my dreamy aspirations and my sobering reality. For starters, the whole routine began in the morning's wee hours, the only time of my average-American day that I could work my ritual—I mean, my Bible reading—into my busy schedule as a wife, mom, interior decorator, and girls' basketball coach. (Granted, those last two occupations seem strange when listed together, but incongruity is another of my lifelong themes!)

Rousing myself from a comfy bed, I'd stumble into the kitchen to grab a Pop-Tart and a glass of milk before opening my Bible to the day's reading. I wasn't necessarily hungry for breakfast, but experience had taught me that nibbling on that Pop-Tart would help to crank up my system, sort of like jump-starting a dead battery. Sadly, once the pastry was consumed, my eyes would begin crossing, and once again, the battle was on! I can still see that sleepy-eyed version of me trying in vain to fend off the drowsiness. More often than not, I left my Bible time as spiritually hungry as I'd come to it, only now I felt defeated as well. Oh, joy. I was reasonably sure this depressing routine didn't qualify as fighting "the good fight of faith" (1 Timothy 6:12), but I simply couldn't seem to summon any energy or enthusiasm for what I was reading.

Sometimes, in a last-ditch effort to focus on the day's Scripture passage, I'd walk around the room while trying to read. This almost worked, but as soon as I grew tired of stumbling in circles (a fitting analogy!) and sat back down, the sleepy monster would grab my eyelids for round two, or three, or four. At least once or twice I actually tried to hold my eyes open *with my fingers* while I read a few more verses! The methods to which I resorted in order to stay awake may seem comical in retrospect, but I couldn't quit trying. As heartbreaking as it was to fail day after day, I knew that God expected me to read His Word, and I really did want to please Him.

Perhaps you recognize the pitiful pattern of those well-intentioned efforts to read the Bible regularly. Maybe it's your present-day ongoing experience, and you'd secretly love to smack people like me who wax on and on about the glories of God's Word. Okay, first off—God doesn't like ugly, so no smacking. But second, you need to know that you don't have an incurable condition. You aren't the first of God's busy kids to fall asleep in class, and you won't be the last. I beg you not to let a little drool on your chin discourage you from experiencing the major transformation awaiting those who discover the Bible's riches.

The turning point for me came when I began to humbly admit to God that I didn't love the Bible. I started by opening my mouth, telling Him that I wanted to love His Word, and asking Him to help birth in me a hunger for it. If the very idea of Bible study intimidates you, I've got super good news. He will meet you in that same confession. One of the first and most important steps you can take in learning to love God's Word is to admit that you don't.

Nothing compares to being personally moved by God's Word. It's good to find stirring devotionals, and it's a blessing to hear inspired preaching, but it has been my experience that they both pale in comparison with meditating on the Word for yourself. Nothing can match feeding at the very Source of life in the intimate discipleship of One-on-one teaching. But then, the fact that you're reading these words suggests you're already sold on the benefits of personal Bible study and meditation. Could it be your problem is more along the lines of how to do it without propping your eyes open with toothpicks? I hear you. I share the memory of my drooling days because I have a burning goal that far outweighs any potential embarrassment: I long to help you learn to feed yourself. I want you to reach that milestone of maturity a whole lot faster than I did, and I'm convinced that you can.

> ### It's good to read stirring devotionals and hear inspired preaching, but both pale in comparison with meditating on the Word for yourself.

It's easy enough to post Scripture on our Facebook status and tweet a daily verse, but God alone knows whether His words truly move us or if they're merely words on a page. Just remember, it's not only acceptable to admit that you don't love to read God's Word, it's recommended. So fess up! There'll be no lightning bolts from the skies, and His feelings won't be hurt by your honesty. Your heavenly Father won't look at Gabriel and exclaim, "Well, have you ever!" God is fully aware of whether you come to the Bible eager to hear from Him or simply to check it off your Good Girl to-do list. Oh, and by the way, He also knows who is skittish about the subject of Bible study because they've suffered on the business end of a Bible beating.

A Bible beating is how I describe the actions of people who use God's words to hurt others or to goad them into empty religious practices. If you suffer from post-traumatic Bible stress, I want you to know that God didn't give us His Word to use as a weapon against one another. Scripture is meant to nourish our souls and equip us to stand against the Evil One.

Take heart, seeker. As surely as our Father knows whether or not we love His Word, and as surely as He knows whether or not someone has used it against us like a hammer, He also knows that not all of us fell wonderfully, mysteriously in love with the Scriptures the moment we came to faith in Him. What's more, He knows that some of us initially tasted the passion only to have lost it somehow along the way.

If you're waiting for God to ease you into a dream state and have you regain consciousness with an insatiable desire to devour the Bible like a pint of cookie-dough ice cream, well, I feel moved to break down yet another hard theological truth for you, in heavy theological-type phrasing: "It ain't happenin', sistah." At least it didn't happen that way for me—or for any of the other passionate students of His Word I've ever met or whose lives I've studied.

> **God is more than willing to morph that hunger into a full-blown addiction for anyone who makes His Word her priority.**

I'll stop short of saying there can't be any testimonies like that out there. I just believe such an experience would be extremely rare! But thankfully, the God who created us, the God who saves us, is the same God who wants to birth in us a hunger for His words. He knows they are "life to those who find them" (Proverbs 4:22). What's more, God is eager to morph that hunger into a full-blown addiction for anyone who makes His Word her priority.

I don't know about you, but just talking about it makes me want to crack the book! Let's look into it now and lay our eyes on a prime example of someone who learned to love God's instruction.

STAKING YOUR OWN CLAIM TO THE TREASURE

I'm sure you've heard of King David, the one-time shepherd boy and musician who became known as the "man after [God's] heart" (Acts 13:22). The Psalms are full of his poetic lyrics about the delights of God's Word.

We tend to imagine David sleeping with a holy scroll from his cradle days, as if he were born with a single-minded commitment to discovering God's ways. Such a conclusion is a colossal mistake. A closer study of the shepherd boy's prayers will yield priceless secrets about David's relationship with God and His Word. We find numerous examples in Psalm 119 alone.

I'd like nothing more than to invite you over for coffee so we could read all one hundred and seventy-six verses together. But since you likely don't have time for an all-day chatfest, I'll rein myself in. Let's begin by listening in on David's prayer in verses 15 and 16. There he is now, strumming his mandolin and declaring his intentions before God:

I will meditate on Your precepts,
And contemplate Your ways.
I will delight myself in Your statutes;
I will not forget Your word. (NKJV)

And there we have our first clue! *This man who grew to love God's Word made an initial decision to value it.* David made it his life's goal to discover God's mysterious ways. It sounds almost too easy, doesn't it? While the rest of us await miraculous moments of biblical inspiration, David spoke of his concrete intentions: "I will meditate. I will contemplate. I will delight. I will not forget." Oh, I love it! How did David come to be so enthralled with God's Word? He chose to value it. He believed there was treasure in God's Word, and he determined not to stop short of discovering as much as he could.

That may sound a lot like my toothpick-in-the-eyes determination, but there is an all-important difference between my approach to God's Word and David's. I was reading it to please God; David was valuing God's ways and His statutes as the treasure they are and staking his claim to them. Big difference!

Bringing God nothing more than a desire to love His Word and a determination to value it is more than enough for Him to work with, as long as we're willing to abandon any and all excuses for not applying ourselves to it and ask Him for help. See if any of these sound familiar.

"The Bible is too hard to understand. I get stuck in the laws and genealogies."

"I don't have time to read the Bible, and besides, I pretty much know what it says."

"I'd like to read the Bible, but I don't know where to start, and no one seems to agree on what it means anyway."

If I missed your favorite line, feel free to jot it in the margins. We need to get those excuses down in black and white so we can strike through them once and for all. (If it will help, think of it as throwing away your fat pants!) Now, with our excuses in full view, let's draw up a "will" like David's and decide, *I will meditate on God's precepts, I will contemplate His ways, I will delight myself in His statutes, and I will remember His words.* Congratulations and whoop, whoop!

SHOW ME THE SIZZLE

Valuing God's Word was just one of David's secrets. Our shepherd king offers us plenty more tips in the same psalm.

In Psalm 119:18 David models another of his characteristic prayers: "Open my eyes that I may see wonderful things in your law" (NIV). At first glance (pun intended), it may seem there's nothing particularly powerful or unusual in this request, but we can ill afford to miss the implication embedded in it—one that strips the devil of another accusation he's been leveling against us for years!

Before and after David's request that God reveal to him the wonders layered in His holy scroll, we find this very same man expounding on the marvelous truths of that very same scroll. For example, "I rejoice in following your statutes as one rejoices in great riches" (verse 14) and "Your statutes are my delight; they are my counselors" (verse 24). So, which is it? Did David find the Word to be marvelous—or did David *want* to find the Word marvelous? The answer is yes and yes. At this point you would be forgiven for thinking both the good king and I are somewhat confused. Let me go at it a different way.

David asked God to open his eyes to the wonder of the Word. God did exactly that—and David's response was to ratchet up the request! Regardless of how much he understood about God and how much treasure he saw in God's ways, David knew still more waited to be uncovered. So he made a practice of asking for his eyes to be opened to further truth. This is one of my favorite David tips! The two-for-one principle has produced delightful results in my own Bible reading. Ask God to show you the wonders in His Word, and don't quit asking! This mind-set and way of praying will put the sizzle in your study.

> Asking God to show you the wonder of His Word, and continuing to ask, will put the sizzle in your study.

Even the quickest glance through the Psalms will prove that David made this type of request of God on a regular basis. In the opening verses of Psalm 119, David extolled the benefits of God's laws and testimonies and then expressed his longing for God to help him keep them.

How blessed are those whose way is blameless,
Who walk in the law of the LORD.
How blessed are those who observe His testimonies,
Who seek Him with all their heart.
They also do no unrighteousness;

They walk in His ways.
You have ordained Your precepts,
That we should keep them diligently.
Oh that my ways may be established
To keep Your statutes! (verses 1–5)

In verse 27 he said, "Let me understand the teaching of your precepts; then I will meditate on your wonders" (NIV). And again in the second half of verse 73, he asked God to "give me understanding to learn your commands" (NIV).

Clearly David knew the dynamite truth that those who regularly ask God to make His Word their delight can expect Him to answer because "those who seek the LORD shall not lack any good thing" (Psalm 34:10, NKJV).

I'm grateful God has answered my initial desperate prayer and birthed in me a love for His Word, but today, tomorrow, and the day after that, you'll find me following David's example, continually asking God to help me love the Scriptures more. I intend to keep asking Him to let me see yet another marvelous truth of His Word that I might truly experience the overflowing wonder of all that is mine through the grace extended to me through Christ Jesus. Just like baby Connor, I want more and I don't mean maybe!

We begin to experience a growing hunger for God's Word when we buy into the truth of Matthew 4:4: "Man shall not live on bread alone, but on every word that proceeds out of the mouth of God." Plenty of people on this planet are breathing in and out, but how many are living as God meant us to live, transformed by passion and fully abandoned to His hand? Will you and I be in that number? We can be. Begin by asking God to help you see the wonders of His Word and keep asking. To pray for God to show you wondrous things in the Bible is to acknowledge that within the pages of Holy

Scripture hides richer treasure than meets the casual observer's eyes—and you're after it!

A TALE OF TWO RATS

Here's a truth that needs to find its way from our heads to our hearts: God's words are irreplaceable. They're a lamp to our feet, light for our path, health to our bodies, refreshment to our bones, and ornaments for our necks (see Psalm 119:105; Proverbs 3:8; 8:11). Reading the Bible isn't one more thing to check off our to-do list to meet some vague quota to satisfy God; it's about feeding our starving souls.

I remember with painful clarity the morning God rocked my well-organized faith with the uncomfortable truth about my checklist approach to time in His Word. I was reading my Bible and saying my prayers because they were my good Christian duties, and I really did want to be a good Christian girl. I know that doesn't sound so bad. But that's only the half of it. What stopped me in my tracks was the realization that time spent in the Bible was my way of *giving God a fix.* Ouch. Ouch. Ouch!

Of course, I wouldn't have called it that. Heavens, no! But however unconsciously it began, and however well meaning my initial intentions, this is precisely what I was doing: giving God just enough of the good stuff to keep Him happy. Devotion? Check. Bible reading? Check. Prayer time? Check. *Are you good now, God? Are we good? Have I given You enough to tide You over for a while?* Ugh. The memory embarrasses me all over again, though I suspect I have plenty of company on this one. How glad I am that God challenged me to face my motives that day and rethink my quiet time quota.

This realization that so often we're just going through the motions brings to mind a story I like to call "A Tale of Two Rats."

My friend Amy had a precocious five-year-old daughter who was already demonstrating that she had personality plus. Amy wrote to tell me that Sarah Caldwell had recently gotten in trouble for disobeying one of her parents' clear rules. As punishment, her dad made her write "I will obey my parents" twenty-five times. The seemingly penitent kindergartner tackled this daunting punishment with great determination—at least at first.

Amy had scanned Sarah Caldwell's finished assignment and attached the file to the e-mail. "Check this out," she said, "and make sure you read all the way to the bottom." My curiosity totally engaged, I opened the attached picture of little Sarah's labors. At the top of the page, in big, fat letters, were her early but earnest efforts at penning out the designated message, "I will obey my parents." Somewhere around line number eleven, however, the child's attention had clearly begun to wander, thus producing another five or six lines of slightly smaller text announcing, "I will obey my arents." Next on the slippery slope came a few lines of "I will obey my rants," all of it leading up to the big finish. The last few lines of Sarah's assignment distinctly read, "I will obey my rats."

When the pleased and penitent Sarah Caldwell turned in the paper, her amused rats made the wise decision not to add any further punishment for her honest mistake. Like Jonathon and Amy, I think Sarah Caldwell's error was purely accidental, the result of her diminishing attention span. Kind of the way you and I can read the Bible without actually hearing the words.

I wonder how many times we think we've met our quota and accomplished something worthwhile with our daily Bible reading when all the time the Father knows we've actually turned in something similar to "I love my rats." Scripture would suggest that if our efforts are geared toward checklists and output, He isn't at all amused by our production.

Consider a few verses from the gospel of John. It's one of the passages God used to speak to me about my own compulsory reading of the great treasure of God's Word. In it Jesus rebuked the Pharisees for an attitude not that much different from our quiet-time quotas: "You diligently study the Scriptures because you think that by them you possess eternal life. These are the Scriptures that testify about me, yet you refuse to come to me to have life" (John 5:39–40, NIV).

> God really would be okay if I didn't get
> His Word in me—I would be the one missing out.

Jesus stood before them, the Word Incarnate. But they preferred to use the Scriptures as tools to justify themselves and condemn others (a.k.a. Bible beatings), rather than to seek out the truth about the Righteous One right there in their midst. In other words, they used the Scriptures as their warranty for righteousness rather than as a window into God's heart.

My previous approach to Bible study fit much the same description. I spent years viewing my time in the Word as something I was doing for God when the wealth between its covers was actually waiting there *for me.* The realization that I had been giving the God of the universe, the Maker and Lover of my soul, a "fix" was painful, but I'm grateful for the wound. It propelled me toward an entirely different relationship with the Bible. Instead of reading for brownie points, I began to see God's Word as the Bread that would keep my spirit from starving and the nutrition that would build the type of faith I longed to experience. I had finally gotten the message: God really would be okay if I didn't get His Word in me—I would be the one missing out!

Following David's example, I began to value the Bible as the place where everything that means anything can be found. As I grasped the reality that feeding on it was God's gift to me and not mine to Him, everything about my experience with the Bible slowly began to change. I started asking the Lord to open my mind to the truth of whatever passage I was reading, and I began taking notes on what I felt the Word was saying to me personally. Instead of waiting contentedly to be fed at the next Sunday sermon, I began to supplement my pastor's good messages with studies from other teachers through print material and audio podcasts, always listening for something I could hold on to and take with me. To my delight, the more stock I put in the value of His Word and the more of it I put in me, the more of it I began to crave.

God is not some vain author who needs us to read his book to inflate his sales numbers. We can't court His favor by plowing our way through the genealogies or meticulously keeping up with our through-the-Bible-in-a-year plan, but all heaven pays attention when we meditate on His holy words and seek to live by them.

THERE'S AN APP FOR THAT!

While the ink's drying on our commitment to feed ourselves from the Good Book, allow me to share a word of caution. Please give yourself permission to begin with a manageable piece of Bread. Resolving to read through the New Testament in a month will only set you up for frustration. I offer you the following testimony from the most unlikely of sources.

My backyard borders a bow-shaped body of water known as Lake Providence. Her manicured banks lined with stately cypress trees nurture all manner of wildlife. One day as I watched a flock of egrets fishing for shad along the lake bank, a certain avian fellow caught my attention. He wasn't any more striking in appearance than his friends; same white feathers, same spindly legs, oblong belly, and beady eyes. It's just that I happened to be looking at him at the exact moment Elvis the Egret won the lottery. (I have a fondness for naming the characters in my stories, and Elvis just felt right for that bird.) While his buddies munched on two-inch shad, Elvis struggled to maintain a tenuous beakhold on the catch of the day. It was a mighty respectable size fish, a record setter on any egret's scale.

Poor Elvis had absolutely zero time for celebration as his catch had brought with it some immediate and pressing concerns. Elvis seemed to be studying the situation even as he fought desperately to better his grip on the constantly flapping fish. I could see right off that tossing his monster prize up and swallowing it whole the way his egret buddies were feeding on their much smaller shad wasn't going to be a viable option. I think he sensed it too.

Elvis made one more valiant effort to reposition his unwieldy prize in the shaky grasp of his beak. Alas, with a well-timed twist, the fish wrenched free, returned to the lake, and swam off, leaving Elvis looking terribly dejected. At least, I imagined he was dejected. To be honest, it's hard to tell with egrets. They don't exactly wear their emotions on their feathers. But seeing as how this is my story, I'll go ahead and add that I also imagined his hunger adding an extra layer of injury to his bruised ego!

The point is not how much of the Bible you get through but how much of the Bible gets through to you!

When it comes to Bible reading, countless people make the same mistake as Elvis the Egret. We attempt to gulp down portions too large to digest. If we try to swallow a humongous passage of God's Word, we'll only end up struggling until we drop it in frustration. Worse, we'll still be hungry, and the Enemy of our souls will make sure we feel defeated, too! It's so much wiser to take a brief passage and approach it reverently and expectantly. The point is not how much of the Bible you get through but how much of the Bible gets through to you! And once you have a little of God's Word in you, you'll discover in your heart a growing desire for more. God's Word is a seed. Plant it. Meditate on it.

I can almost hear you now: "All right, Shellie! I'm right there with you, but what does this meditating look like exactly, and better yet, how do I get there from here?"

One of the most meaningful ways I've found to meditate expectantly on God's Word is to take a small portion of Scripture and ask the Holy Spirit to teach me from it. (My church girls might even say I obsess about a passage, and they may be speaking the truth!) I'll read my current verse or verses, ponder what I've read, and set out to memorize it. If you involuntarily flinched when I said the word *memorize,* do stay with me. It's no time for despair. This is a lot more doable than you may have made it out to be.

You know that cell phone that rides on your hip or in your purse, the one that's never far from your side lest you have a fit and fall in it? (Okay, perhaps that last part was self-revelatory.) I like to type my current Scripture focus into the notepad on my smartphone so I can reread it in small snatches of time throughout the day. A host of Bible apps are available for free downloading, and some have audio capabilities. I've learned to use one of these to bookmark my Scripture focus for easy listening during my daily walks or while running errands. Even better, my smartphone came with a voice memo recorder into which I sometimes speak the scripture so I can play it back in my own voice. The point is, the more we involve our senses in memorization, the easier it becomes. Read it, type it, write it, and listen to it! (Oh, and do e-mail me when you become pleasantly surprised by how well you're doing!)

This process of embracing a passage, memorizing it, and squeezing abundant life out of it can be done just as well with a legal pad and a pile of books. Shorthand, longhand, or typing hands, choose your pleasure.

I like to memorize, study, and meditate on a single passage for one week or several months, rehearsing it in my heart and with my lips as often as I can. I'll ask the Holy Spirit to open my eyes to what I'm seeing and my ears to what I'm hearing, and I'll trust the greatest Teacher the world could ever know to reveal truth from what I'm reading. What I will not do any longer is read for reading's sake. No more quiet-time quotas for me!

Another life-transforming study habit I've developed is talking back to the Scriptures. I can't encourage you strongly enough to audibly respond to what you're reading. You do know that John 1:1 tells us Jesus is the Word and the Word is Jesus, right? In describing Jesus, Revelation 19:13 says, "He is clothed with a robe dipped in blood, and His name is called The Word of God." This being the case, I implore you to begin talking back to Him.

I like to read a verse of Scripture and ask out loud, "Lord, what are you saying to me here?" Then I'll sit for a moment or two and wait. Sometimes another scripture drops into my heart. Sometimes a word in the first verse that hadn't captured my attention before will suddenly stand out and prompt me to take a closer look, researching its definition or looking it up in one of my commentaries. Often the definition in one commentary will lead me to another verse that feels very much like a continuing dialogue with the first passage.

> God's Word moves those
> who give themselves to it.

Do I hear something every time I stop and ask like this? Absolutely not! Sometimes I'll be led to another verse immediately and sometimes I won't. At times an answer will come much later, but that's good too! When His words drop into my heart unexpectedly, they're the sweetest of surprises or the timeliest of instructions.

Our willingness to pause and interact with the Bible and meditate on God's words allows them to become life to our spirits. The Word of God moves those who give themselves to it. Listen to these verses from Proverbs 2, and hear God encouraging anyone who will search the Scriptures as if mining for gold.

My son, if you receive my words,

And treasure my commands within you,

So that you incline your ear to wisdom,

And apply your heart to understanding;

Yes, if you cry out for discernment,

And lift up your voice for understanding,

If you seek her as silver,

And search for her as *for* hidden treasures;

Then you will understand the fear of the L ORD,

And find the knowledge of God....

When wisdom enters your heart,

And knowledge is pleasant to your soul,

Discretion will preserve you;

Understanding will keep you. (verses 1–5, 10–11, NKJV)

No other book lives and breathes as the Bible does. Engage the Author and listen. Ask Him to let you hear His voice and feel His breath in its pages.

YOU'VE REALLY GOT A HOLD ON ME

Sometimes I use my evening walk to think further on a particular Scripture passage while jamming to some good worship music (Go, Babbie!) or to catch up on my favorite Bible study podcasts (Yea, Beth!). One day I had my earbuds in and the volume dialed up when I was suddenly and unexpectedly set free.

I'd been bopping along and watching Dixie Belle, my famously rotten chocolate Lab, running a hundred yards ahead of me, when an ultrasneaky German shepherd tiptoed up behind me and stuck his cold, wet nose against the inside of my bare leg. Hallelujah and praise the Lord, I almost went home to see Jesus right there! As I pulled myself together, I noted that sneaky canine varmint taking the opportunity to adjourn to a nearby ditch to either roll around in something dead or give himself permission to fall down and laugh out loud.

> Every single choice we make
> to take hold of Scripture provides another
> opportunity for Scripture to grab hold of us.

For anyone trying to live the Christ life apart from the steady nourishment of the Word, the brevity of that freeing experience stands as a pretty good metaphor. Consider the words of John 8:31–32: "To the Jews who had believed him, Jesus said, 'If you hold to my teaching, you are really my disciples. Then you will know the truth, and the truth will set you free'" (NIV). Please note that Jesus gave this promise of freedom to the Jews *who had already come to believe in Him.* Jesus came to the world to show humanity the truth—Himself, God in human form—and an encounter with Him will most assuredly set us free. But if that encounter stops with an introductory meeting, our freedom won't last that much longer than my incident with Mr. Sneaky. Jesus said He is "the way, and the truth, and the life" (John 14:6). We need an ongoing experience with Him to walk in the freedom He offers—and we can have it through the Word.

Every single choice we make to take hold of Scripture provides another opportunity for Scripture to grab hold of us. I know because it happened to me. How well I remember forcing myself to scan enough verses to check off Bible reading on the daily to-do list and giving myself the "day off" on Saturdays. (We'd be in church the next day, after all.) It's hard to believe *that* me is the same one who simply can't get enough of the Word today. It's not unusual for me to complete my own time in the Bible and head to my bedroom to shower and get ready for the day, only to turn on the television as soon as

I dry off so I can hear more good teaching while I dress and do my makeup. Yes, I do have to turn it up sky high to hear it over my blow-dryer, and yes, my man does say someone could slip up on me and I'd never hear 'em coming, but Jesus has my back.

Sometimes I stand amazed at how addicted I've become to the Bible. And yet it proves a great truth that I hope will encourage you in your pursuit of All Things Jesus: we become hungry for what we feed on, and the more we feed on God and His Word, the more of Him we crave.

David, Did You Drool?

How about one more tip from King David? I can't resist. That's him over there praying. If we lean in, we can hear him talking to God:

> Incline my heart to Your testimonies,
> And not to covetousness.
> Turn away my eyes from looking at worthless things,
> And revive me in Your way. (Psalm 119:36–37, NKJV)

Promise me you won't miss the power of this one! In asking God to incline his heart to His testimonies, the king admits that his heart isn't *always* turned to God's Word. According to David's own confession, sometimes it's turned to the things of this world. We have indeed happened upon the king in a most vulnerable moment!

Did you notice how closely David's prayer resembles the one that opens our chapter? Take away the ancient Hebrew phrasing, and you get roughly the same sentiment: *"I want to love your Word, God, but I don't. Help me learn to hunger for Your truth!"*

Here's our super-duper Bible-loving friend confessing that he needs God to transform the natural inclination of his heart, turning it from the things of this world to a desire for God's testimonies! Could it be that David's scroll had a bit of drool on it? And, dare I say it, maybe the parchment even gathered a little cave dust or castle cobwebs from time to time? Apparently so. And yet this is the man with the famous reputation we were admiring earlier, the one about whom God said, "I have found David the son of Jesse, a man after My heart" (Acts 13:22). Let that encourage you. It does me.

I find it strangely comforting that David prayed the same way thousands of years before we stumbled into our own why-don't-I-love-the-Bible predicament. I'm grateful that God chose to let us see David's honesty. I hear him asking God to make him want the right things, and I can relate. Our conflicted king was simply admitting that even after enjoying the unequaled treasures of God's good Word, he could still find himself indifferent to its wonder! Our poster boy recognized in himself the tendency to value what this world offers, as evidenced by that tagged-on request to turn his heart from worthless pursuits! That's encouragement to someone who occasionally finds herself in the same quandary.

Girlfriend, I need you to know that the prayers in this book are not prayers I once prayed. I still pray them all the time, and I don't intend to stop! The Word has truly become Bread to me, and I'm fully convinced of how desperately I need its constant guidance and nourishment. I know I can't live on yesterday's reading, and I have no desire to live on old bread! And yet I also know how vulnerable my heart remains to being tempted, torn, and divided. It's why a version of David's prayer is always on my lips.

Lord, help me love Your Word more, always more. Keep turning my heart to the Bible. If You don't fan the flame of my desire, I'm afraid it will sputter out while I chase worthless things. Give me a preference for Your Word over any other instruction. Make it my favorite book! Shift my heart to Your ways and away from the ways of the world. Help me love Your Word and prefer it! Amen.

4

DOES GOD WANT OUT OF OUR QUIET TIMES?

"Lord, teach me how to live devoted beyond
my daily devotional."

As a teenager I often daydreamed about what it would have been like to attend a ball in the Old South with my dance card attached to my gloved wrist. I could see myself penciling in the eager suitors vying for my attention while I fanned myself and smoothed the fabric of my big old hoop skirt, à la Scarlett from *Gone with the Wind*. Never you mind that my southern roots trace closer to the barefoot kids on nearby sharecropping farms than to the well-heeled party goers on a storied plantation— dance cards spoke romance to my adolescent heart. I'd read enough about them in books and I'd seen enough old movies to know they spoke volumes about their owners too. Sketchy dance cards were to be pitied, while a full program declared a belle's status as a superpopular dancing machine.

You and I don't have dance cards, of course. But if we're honest, sometimes we can be similarly proud of our booked-up day planners and digital calendars, even as we profess to be exhausted by the pace we're keeping.

We're familiar with the Father's invitation to "be still, and know that I am God" (Psalm 46:10, NIV). Our problem is slowing down from all the doing to practice the being without getting mowed down by all our other commitments. The idea of running after God sounds great—if we weren't already slap out of breath. Do I hear a tired amen?

I get it, girlfriend! I've been known to try to squeeze God into that brief lull between dances too. It doesn't work, does it? Trying to live for Jesus without living with Jesus leaves a girl as out of sorts as the concrete angel who once lived on my back porch.

She was a tiny thing, my angel, and a busy one. She spent her days perched on the side of my fountain, pouring water from the small basin in her delicate hands into the stained-glass pool beneath her feet. She was sweet enough—if I tended to her properly. But I'll be straight with you, the girl had her moments. My angel's water supply had a tendency to evaporate in the heat of our long Delta days. If I remembered to replenish it regularly, my angel and her overflowing basin charmed me with the most pleasing background music as I sat on the porch and wrote. But let her water level drop too low, and the delicate winged one turned into a banshee—a screeching, grating, obnoxious shrew, her pump desperately sucking air where water should be. When that happened, the girl destroyed whatever tenuous tranquility existed.

> The idea of running after God sounds great—
> if we aren't already slap out of breath.

I see myself in that story. If you'll look at the reflection, you may recognize someone you know.

Jesus said, "If anyone is thirsty, let him come to me and drink. Whoever believes in me, as the Scripture has said, streams of living water will flow from within him" (John 7:37–38, NIV). Jesus offers more than a drink of water to quench our physical thirst. He offers streams of living water to satisfy the deep drought of our souls through the gift of His indwelling Spirit.

His words depict a flow of life-giving water that is always available for the one who learns to resort to the well.

What's more, Jesus says we can carry this fountain about in our own lives. But note the progression. When we go to God for nourishment, His heavenly H$_2$O fills us up and flows back out from us in a pleasing melody that falls refreshingly on our family and friends. And yet, like the angel in my water fountain, when we fail to replenish ourselves at the Source, our faith talk sounds hollow to this hurting world at best and like grating Christianese at worst.

I can almost hear you saying, "Okay, I agree with you, Shellie, but you should see my schedule. I just don't see where I can find the time to do anything about it." Hang on tight, y'all. My goal for this chapter isn't about making you feel so guilty that you set your alarm for three o'clock in the morning and prop your eyes open with those toothpicks we have already decided to trash. Nor am I looking to help you be a better organizer so you can carve out a whole new block of time in your day. Frankly, my intentions dwarf those. I'm hoping to turn the way you're looking at this time-for-God thing upside down. I'm officially asking you to give up your quiet time.

A QUIET TIME? FORGET ABOUT IT!

I wish I could see your face right now. Give up your quiet time?! The very suggestion has a whiff of heresy.

A myriad of sermons and volumes of books have declared the importance of setting aside a regular time of personal devotion to Bible study and prayer. Through modern church history, this practice has been called by various names, including The Daily Watch, The Morning Hour, or Time of Meditation. Before anyone comes after me with a switch, let me be clear. I'm all for the worthy goal of prioritizing time to pursue God's holy presence. I just want us to quit checking off our quiet time as if it's one more appointment in the day planner.

Having a quiet time shouldn't be the end goal, but sometimes our routines suggest it is. We carve out a block of time and go through our checklist of reading and prayer while the clock ticks away. If we're "successful"—if we manage to stay with it until our time is up—we congratulate ourselves and get on with the real business of the day. And all the while we wonder why we don't more intimately know the God who chose us, redeemed us, and promises to give us life in its fullest measure.

Heaven help us.

The One who holds our breath in His hand desires our company. If the mission of our quiet times is to know Him, I have a sweeping suggestion: instead of trying to find time in our day for God, let's determine to find God throughout our day.

We can set aside routine times to read the Bible and pray, and we can stencil His words on our walls, but if we want to know the One who speaks them, we need to invite Him into what I fondly call the Marvelous Mundane.

> Instead of trying to find time in our day for God, I'm suggesting our goal should be finding God throughout our day.

My small hometown's annual Fourth of July celebration has become a family tradition. We douse ourselves with mosquito repellant until the chemicals hang in the air, stinging our eyes and lingering in our mouths, in hopes of holding off the munching mosquitoes of the Louisiana Delta long enough to witness the community fireworks. We load up on a float boat with friends and motor out to the middle of beautiful Lake Providence, joining a host of other vessels trolling slowly in anticipation of the big over-the-water display.

Sometimes we wave at passing boatloads of quiet, shadowy onlookers we can't identify as well as the other not-so-quiet revelers like ourselves who are more recognizable. The vocally challenged in our group, of which I am first and foremost, join the more musically inclined to croon a few lively patriotic tunes. Finally, the clock strikes the magic moment and exploding colors begin to burst from a platform in the middle of the lake, brightening the night sky and eliciting oohs and aahs across land and water.

> We've all been guilty of trading
> the marvelous for the mundane.

One year as I watched the fireworks build toward the finale, I found myself wondering how many of our small town's residents were missing the show. I figured the odds were good that some people were hunkered down in their homes with the TV blaring, their poor substitute turned up a few extra notches to drown out the celebratory noise. It may sound ridiculous for anyone to miss such an awesome night, but at some level we're all guilty of trading the marvelous for the mundane.

We hunker down and forge through our activities while the One the Bible calls the Morning Star pulls out all the stops to display His glory and reveal Himself in us and around us every day (see 2 Peter 1:19). If we relegate God to the parameters of our devotional times, we will miss the joy of walking with Him in the Marvelous Mundane of our lives. (By the way, I hear tell He has a finale planned that is literally out of this world.)

A LESSON FROM A HOOT OWL

I can remember occasions when my morning quiet time was interrupted by a child's cry or the ring of the telephone and I would actually think to myself,

Oh well. That's it for today. I'll try to "find" God again tomorrow. (If you laughed it means you've done it too.)

If only we could grasp this truth: every moment (that means this one right now) is a brand-new opportunity to experience the hope of glory, Christ in us (see Colossians 1:27). That includes standing in line at Starbucks, checking out at the grocery store, and fighting traffic on the freeway. He speaks in every moment.

Once I decided to let God out of my quiet time and into the rest of my day, I began to hear Him speaking to me from all directions. That invitation is one I still extend to the Lord regularly. As I close my Bible or end my early morning prayers, I like to tell Him that I have no desire to leave His sweet company. I don't want to walk out of prayer; I want to walk in prayer. I ask God to continue to speak to me throughout the day and to give me ears to hear Him and eyes to see Him. Oh, can I tell you that He is faithful to such a request!

I might be driving along and see a road sign for a rest area ahead, and He will remind me of His offer: "Come to Me, all who are weary and heavy-laden, and I will give you rest" (Matthew 11:28).

I can be traveling alone, lost in a crowd of people, and suddenly remember that He has written *my* name on His palms (see Isaiah 49:16), and I'll hear those words as a divine invitation to connect with Him. Sometimes I can stop and pray. Other times all I might be able to do in response is to utter a simple, quiet "Hello, Father" or "Thank You, Jesus," but that's okay too! My heart has turned toward Him, and I'm reminded that I am not alone. He is with me. The more I invite God into my whole day, the more I find bits of Scripture and thoughts of Him coming to me like shots of spiritual adrenaline.

For instance, I doubt you would notice the faded marks on my chest if you were with me right now, but I can still see them. I know where to look.

I call these marks my love wounds, gifts from my youngest grandchild. It's unintentional, for sure, this habit baby Connor has of playing with your skin while you're holding him close. He doesn't pinch. He just likes to, well, fiddle with you, for lack of a better word. Connor doesn't understand the scratches his baby fingernails leave behind.

As strange as this is going to sound, I've found it sad to watch those marks fade. Connor lives in Texas. I don't get to see him as often as I would like, and I miss him. My scars are love wounds that remind me of Connor and keep me in a state of anticipation about seeing him again. Their tender appeal for me is born out of my love for the one who marked me. And yes, they provide a tailor-made moment to see and worship God.

In being purposeful about mining everyday life for sights of Jesus, my thoughts can progress to another set of love wounds—the scars in His hands and His feet, the wounds on His brow, His back, and His side. It's been two thousand plus years since our sins marred the body of Jesus Christ, and praise God, they haven't faded! The Holy Scriptures tell us that one day we will look upon that blessed body that was pierced for you and for me, and what a glorious day that will be (see John 19:37). I love to consider this compelling thought: when Jesus arose from the grave and returned to heaven, He came home to His Father and ours with a glorified body bearing evidence of His love for you and me. Can we even imagine all of heaven being able to see those scars that never fade, declaring eternal love for those He died to save? When He sees them, He sees us. It's okay if that makes you want to shout. I have. This practice of looking for Him in the moments of our lives will do that.

Does using the word *practice* to describe seeking God sound dry and ritualistic to you? I hope not. To practice simply means to do something repeatedly and intentionally toward a predetermined goal. If the objective of our practice sessions is to know God, we can expect a supernatural payoff. Remember our earlier discussion that ours isn't a God "out there" but a God "right here." God doesn't play hard to get or hide-and-seek. He simply waits for us to tear our eyes away from our smartphones or to-do lists long enough to look purposefully for Him. And when we do, He promises that our efforts will be rewarded.

Scripture teaches that something amazing happens when we become intentional and determined about looking for God.

> Blessed are they who keep his statutes and seek him with all their heart. (Psalm 119:2, NIV)

> You will seek Me and find Me when you search for Me with all your heart. (Jeremiah 29:13)

> If you seek Him, He will be found by you. (1 Chronicles 28:9, NKJV)

God desires our company more than we want His. That's why, when we ask, He'll help us develop this habit of looking for Him throughout our day.

The exciting possibilities of practicing this divine search were brought home to me through a hoot owl, of all things. At the time the owl was nesting somewhere on our property. Bless his heart, he was one confused creature. I could hear the poor thing calling out in the daylight hours when everyone knows good little owls are supposed to be napping. Trying to catch a glimpse of him, I followed his "hootie-hoo" call all over our property, to no avail. The sound seemed to come from the backyard and the front yard at the same time.

After weeks of this, my husband and I were having our early morning coffee together when he pointed toward the window.

"There's your owl," he said casually. I looked and saw nothing.

"Right there," Phil said again.

This time I positioned myself behind him and followed his pointing finger carefully. He was right! Barely visible in the predawn light, my owl was resting high in a cypress tree on the lake bank, surrounded by branches and foliage. I never would've spotted him had Phil not pointed him out.

"How on earth did you see him?" I asked.

My man shrugged. "It's a hunting thing. My eyes are trained to notice anything out of the ordinary."

I bet you see where I'm going, but I'll be happy to spell it out. Sometimes we act as if we can't see God or hear God the way other people can, as if our faith is disabled, when we simply haven't trained ourselves to look and listen. If that resonates with you, let me encourage you with the prayer Paul prayed over his friends at Philippi: "And this I pray, that your love may abound yet more and more in real knowledge and all discernment" (Philippians 1:9).

If you've ever felt a desire to know God, you've felt God move. If you are hungry to know God, you've heard Him call. With His help we can learn to recognize His voice and see His hand at work.

> ### If you've ever felt a desire to know God, you've felt God move.

One of the sweetest by-products of the habit is that when we see Him, we can point Him out for others, just as Phil and his hunter's eyesight helped me spot my owl.

RUN, FORREST, RUN!

The life devoted to finding God learns the blessedness of an ongoing interaction with Him, whether we're on our knees in prayer or en route to a T-ball game. It involves having our hearts turned toward heaven even when our eyes are on a computer screen or our hands are busy in the kitchen. This should be our default mode, and we need to be willing and eager to reset as often as necessary. I think of this as the spiritual equivalent of the phrase, "Run, Forrest, run!"

You may remember that line from the 1994 movie *Forrest Gump*. The main character, Forrest, stole our collective hearts with his friendliness and loyalty. After a childhood spent with braces on his legs, Forrest shucked his shackles early in the movie to outrun a group of bullies. In the course of that escape, Forrest accidentally discovered that he could run—and run fast!

From then on, Forrest ran in one challenging situation after another. As a matter of fact, not only did he rescue himself, but his willingness to run began to figure into the rescue of others who were dear to him. There's such a great lesson here. Forrest's example can remind us to run to God and cry for help at the first hint of trouble and then keep running back whenever we find anxiety threatening to return.

Consider the following scenario: One morning the planets line up, the husband and kids cooperate, and you actually have a period of uninterrupted time with Jesus. It feels like balm for your soul! You are able to pray about a certain problem and exchange your despair for hope that God has heard your cries. For a time after that, peace reigns in your heart.

Unfortunately, at some point later in the day, the troubling merry-go-round of thoughts starts up again, and you're in danger of falling right back into the familiar rut of despair. Now you have a choice. You can try thinking about something else, which is always a losing battle (do not think about a chocolate chip cookie right now). You can choose to give in to the despair. Bad idea! Or you can choose to run. You can run back to God as fast as your spiritual legs can carry you to acknowledge your weakness and your need for His strength. You might cry out verbally or silently, whatever the setting allows, but the vital thing is to humble yourself and call out honestly, "It's me again, Lord! I need more hope. Mine has leaked out once again!"

It's been my experience that often we don't realize when our thoughts have strayed from God or when they've returned to their defeated looping pattern. That's why I make a practice of telling the Lord that I want Him in all my thoughts! I repeat that prayer daily, and I can testify that He is showing me His faithfulness in this area.

Other times we simply fail to understand how desperately we need Him day in and day out—or we seek God's help for the big hairy problems while deciding our everyday stuff is too trivial to take to Him. Neither of those lines of reasoning passes the smell test of Scripture.

Fortify your resolve to resort to Him yet again with these words:

Through the LORD's mercies we are not consumed,
Because His compassions fail not.
They are new every morning;
Great is Your faithfulness. (Lamentations 3:22–23, NKJV)

God's love for you is constant. Far from being used up, today's mercies have barely even been tried. Return His embrace and you will find Him faithful to forgive, renew, and lead you into abundant life.

Psalm 139 contains another reassuring reminder of just how interested our God is in whatever concerns us. Read it and reread it until the truth settles in your soul.

O LORD, you have searched me
    and you know me.
You know when I sit and when I rise;
    you perceive my thoughts from afar.
You discern my going out and my lying down;
    you are familiar with all my ways.

Before a word is on my tongue
  you know it completely, O LORD.
You hem me in—behind and before;
  you have laid your hand upon me.
Such knowledge is too wonderful for me,
  too lofty for me to attain. (verses 1–6, NIV)

Celebrate that passage with me a moment. Those words don't paint the picture of a distant God who would berate us for needing Him. I hope this doesn't sound flippant, but God is clearly *into* His kids. What do you need right now? What does your family need? Run, Forrest, *run*!

PURSUIT TRUMPS PERFORMANCE

Choosing this ongoing awareness and acknowledgment of God in our everyday moments transforms our lives because we humans have only two settings: we're either acknowledging God or we're looking to be acknowledged ourselves. Living for the applause of people will be the experience of everyone who doesn't purposely choose to live for God, because the human heart craves attention.

One night I watched a man on a television talent show dive from a twenty-foot platform into twelve inches of water. Not only did he survive the experience, but he promised afterward that if the judges would send him on to the next round, he would dive from even greater heights in weeks to come! I could almost imagine him speaking on behalf of the entire human race. "I'll run faster, jump higher, and write more books; just pick me. Acknowledge me."

I find it both fascinating and sad to consider how desperate many people are to be acknowledged, for someone to know that they lived, breathed, and died. It's the misguided quest of every human heart, but we were born for more. The fullest life is found in acknowledging God and living to shout His fame. Receiving acclaim for ourselves feels good and is temporarily satisfying, but be warned: praise never fulfills the Me-Monster. A little recognition is like an addictive drug. It only makes us want more. We could list a string of celebrities as exhibits of what this human tendency looks like when it's indulged, but I think we've seen enough public train wrecks to get the point without the name calling.

> The misguided quest of every human heart
> is the need to be acknowledged, but the
> fullest life is found in acknowledging God.

The practice of acknowledging God and living for Him rather than struggling to be known for our own accomplishments frees us from the need to jump from the highest platform or swim the deepest sea for the world's approval, and it carries the promise of enjoying His sweet presence—whether or not we've had a quiet time that morning!

I'm excited about sharing more concrete ideas on how we can watch for God throughout our days, but first let me quickly remind you and me both to be careful not to confuse pursuing God with performing for God! We simply can't log enough hours in our relationship with God to earn the right to approach Him. Jesus is and will always be the Door to both initial access to God and a continual relationship with Him: "In him and through faith in him we may approach God with freedom and confidence" (Ephesians 3:12, NIV). But the lies of the Enemy often keep us from enjoying this privilege. We'll take a closer look at the trap of "performance religion" in chapter 6, because anyone who tries to walk in the presence of God faces it. For our purposes right now, let's just note that if Satan isn't reminding us of what we've done wrong, he's reminding us of what we haven't done right!

This most often sounds like self-talk. We don't hear the Enemy say, "*You haven't prayed in a week. What good is it to pray today?*" If he did, we might actually recognize his trap and hightail it to our Father. (Run, Forrest, run!) No, that would be too obvious. Instead we hear what we think is our own hearts saying, "*I haven't prayed all week. What difference could another day make?*" And with that we voluntarily forfeit God's divine companionship and grow weaker when we could've relied on Him to grow stronger! If you haven't been inviting God into your day, begin to do so right now. Don't let the Enemy trick you into making a bad situation worse.

The other day, during an intimate conversation with a small circle of women in the corner of a busy coffee shop, I asked one of my girlfriends how she was doing. She knew I was asking about her desire to know God, which was the purpose behind my regular meetings with these young women, all of them hungry for heaven.

"Not good at all," she said. "I mean, I want to pray and I'll try to pray… but then I'll go days without praying or reading my Bible and…"

When her voice trailed off, I pressed gently, "And?"

A torrent of words rushed out honestly and painfully. "And then something happens and I know I need to pray, but I don't feel like I have the right to because I haven't been praying!"

My heart broke for my friend. I recognized the pattern of guilt. Some of my memories are comical, others are downright embarrassing, but since I've already confessed to propping my eyes open to read the Bible, I might as well tell you about the pathetic approach to prayer I once used. It's worth it to me if it will help you take a running jump into the arms of Jesus and skip some of the melodrama I endured, feeling my way in the dark, bumping into chairs and stubbing my toes while wondering why He couldn't talk *just a teensy-weensy bit louder.*

"Jesus, If You're There, Please Make the Lights Blink"

When I was a little girl, my sisters and I often joined our cousins to hold séances like those we saw in the made-for-television movies. We'd turn off the overhead light and place a shirt over the night-light to set just the right mood. I distinctly remember we found it difficult to decide who exactly we wanted to call back from the dead. More than likely this was because we were too young to know many people who had passed on. But eventually we would decide on a potential guest, and our séance would commence.

We would gather in a circle, hold hands, adopt the most respectful posture possible, and ask our guest to show that he or she was there with us by "performing." We didn't call it performing, mind you, but that's what it was. We wanted our supernatural visitor to move a chair, turn on the light, or open the door—anything to prove that he or she was listening. As far as waiting on the dead goes, our attention span was limited. If he or she didn't "show up" in record time, we would move on to the next game on our agenda, signaling to our would-be guest that (a) our heart wasn't in it in the first place, and (b) we couldn't be expected to wait around all day with our eyes closed! We had other games to play. It was also a deal breaker if Mama called to us from the other part of the house or if she, heaven forbid, opened the door to our room. Game over, or rather, séance over. To overstate the obvious, we didn't know jack squat about what we were doing and that alone makes the memory a most fitting analogy for my purposes.

The truth is, my prayer times used to look quite similar to those childhood séances. I had my own prayer procedures, and I followed them like a superstitious athlete checking off game-day rituals. Any deviation from the system could break the mood and signal game over, or rather prayer time over.

My carefully crafted formula for prayer time started with a perfectly quiet room. Best case scenario—meaning that which was most conducive to a successful séance—none of my family members were home when I reached out to the heavenly throne. But if totally private time wasn't possible, which was most often the case, the next best situation was for the rest of the household to be asleep. There were other predictors of whether or not I would have a successful prayer time. I prayed "best" if I sang a few songs, preferably beginning with fast ones and then moving to slow ones. And I believed I was more likely to connect with God in a meaningful way after I had read a good portion of the Scriptures to set the mood. Please tell me you're laughing because you can relate!

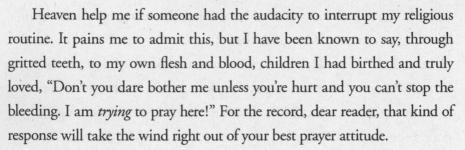

My prayer times once followed my own carefully crafted formula—for failure!

Heaven help me if someone had the audacity to interrupt my religious routine. It pains me to admit this, but I have been known to say, through gritted teeth, to my own flesh and blood, children I had birthed and truly loved, "Don't you dare bother me unless you're hurt and you can't stop the bleeding. I am *trying* to pray here!" For the record, dear reader, that kind of response will take the wind right out of your best prayer attitude.

On a good séance day, the kids would leave me alone and the phone wouldn't ring off the hook and I could proceed in my efforts to "reach" the throne. I do hope you're picking up the sarcasm I'm laying down. I didn't consider what I was doing to be a séance. Far from it! I was utterly sincere, just woefully misguided or tragically uninformed. Take your pick. The result was the same: a feeling of hopelessness over my inability to pray joined at the hip with guilt, my ever-present companion.

Oh, friend, do you see the trap? Let's forget what is behind—forget our failed attempts at perfection and our pathetic list of prerequisites for prayer—and press on to what is ours in Christ (see Philippians 3:13–14)! Let's not wait for devotional time but talk to Him whenever and wherever we can. He's waiting to hear from us.

> For thus says the Lord GOD, the Holy One of Israel:
> "In returning and rest you shall be saved;
> In quietness and confidence shall be your strength."
> But you would not. (Isaiah 30:15, NKJV)

PRAYER: THE LONG AND SHORT OF IT

Let's recap. Instead of looking for time in our day for God, we've decided to look for God all through our day. We've decided to run to Jesus to find hope for our troubled hearts and return to Him as often as we need a booster shot! What's more, we've determined not to succumb to guilt or let our Enemy trick us out of God's company. Instead, we'll celebrate His endless mercy and compassion and the steadfast love that welcomes us back every single time.

Now that we're chasing hard after God's companionship, we'll find a myriad of ways to weave devotion into the rhythm of our daily lives and not just within our quiet times. As we do, we'll want to remember to use our words, all of them. Not just the dressed-up ones we used this morning in our devotional time, the words that seemed so holy. You know, back when we were actually feeling spiritual, before the school called *again,* before our best friend hurt our feelings, and before the nice policeman felt it necessary to write that ticket. (Wait. That last one might have been for me.)

"Use your words" is a line I've adopted as one of my prayer mottos after seeing my daughter and daughter-in-law employ the phrase with my grand-children. I was watching once when my daughter said, "Use your words," to my first grandson, Grant Thomas. He stopped crying, thought really hard, twisted up his adorable toddler face, and said, "Kwacker." I, of course, clapped as if he had just delivered the Gettysburg Address without a teleprompter, then promptly zoomed to the pantry to get him a cracker for each hand.

For the most part, Grant Thomas responded well when he was reminded to "use your words." So did his cousin, Emerson Ann. I remember my daughter-in-law using the same tactic to ward off one of Emerson's meltdowns. Watching Jessica and Carey convinced me that this line was a lot nicer than the one I had used years earlier on my own kids. "Hush up that crying" wasn't nearly as effective at getting to the root of the problem. Sometimes it seems that all the little ones really need is to be reminded that they are whining.

That goes for big ones too. We tend to operate under a similar default setting. Let our little red wagon get turned over, and our first instinct is to mumble, grumble, and whine. If you want to stay in touch with your Father throughout the day, make a habit of using your words, your prayer words. When life pushes your frustration button, turn to Him and use your words. If you're sad, turn to Him and use your words. Don't try to form a King James English prayer suitable for Westminster Abbey. Simply run to Jesus, the Lover of your soul, tell Him how you feel, and ask for help to deal with whatever you're facing. He wants to be brought smack-dab into your Marvelous Mundane, remember?

Here's just one of the many upsides to using your words with God. Sometimes He'll use your own words to speak to you about the heart of the problem. What you think is bothering you may not be the real issue at all! I call it the lesson of the big black purse.

Not long ago I was digging around in my purse for a lost earring when I finally gave up and dumped the entire contents out on my bed. Surprise! I found the missing earring and a host of other things I didn't know were in there. Psalm 62:8 tells us, "Pour out your hearts to him, for God is our refuge" (NIV). Heeding this biblical admonition to pour out our hearts in prayer can have the same benefits as unloading our purses (or briefcases or hunting bags). Sometimes we don't know what's in our hearts until we empty them. We simply need to learn when and where to dump 'em.

> **Use your words. Sometimes we don't know what's in our hearts until we empty them.**

God stands ready to help us sort through our stuff, but we often resort to unloading our hearts on other people instead. Whether or not we do this consciously, many of us have been guilty of illegal dumping.

I once found myself driving behind a pickup truck that was steadily littering my beautiful Louisiana. When the first piece of trash flew out of his truck bed, I winced and chalked it up to accidental negligence. A little farther down the road, a fast-food bag escaped, followed by a Styrofoam cup. That's when I began to wonder just how clueless he was. That litterbug may have been in the dark, or it could be that he didn't care. I've seen news reports of people who secretly dump loads of trash in rural areas (as if it didn't happen if no one saw them doing it). That's downright nervy and sad.

Both negligent littering and illegal dumping speak volumes. For starters, they say the guilty party is unwilling to take the time or expend the effort necessary to put his or her trash where it belongs. Likewise, the Bible teaches that there is a right way and a wrong way to handle our emotional messes. "Be anxious for nothing, but in everything by prayer and supplication with thanksgiving let your requests be made known to God. And the peace of God, which surpasses all comprehension, will guard your hearts and your minds in Christ Jesus" (Philippians 4:6–7).

Everyone feels the occasional need to talk things through with a flesh-and-blood person, but it shouldn't be because we haven't taken or won't take the time to dispose of our feelings correctly by taking them to our Father. God can handle our ranting, but frankly, sharing our issues with another person sometimes morphs into illegal dumping, as such venting often serves no greater purpose than to depress both us and our listeners. Most of the time, all a human listener can do is listen, even if he or she would like to do more. By contrast, pouring out our hearts to God brings the problem before the One who sees it from every angle. He can work everything out according to His divine purposes while bringing peace right into the middle of our emotional meltdowns.

Of course, just as our interactions with God aren't meant to be restricted to a devotional time, neither should they be reserved for times of crisis or the need to rant; sometimes we just need a Jesus fix. Our thoughts might turn to God in the middle of the day and we'll find ourselves longing to connect, but there's no way to retreat from a crying baby, two toddlers, and a boiling pot of peas. For these moments I highly recommend the "That's All I've Got" method of prayer. The name came about through a particular style of conversation I've developed with my daughter.

Let me be clear: I'm not at all happy about living on opposite ends of the earth from my married daughter, but I'm learning to deal with it. Okay, so I live in northeast Louisiana and she's one state over in Houston, Texas. Let's not get bogged down in the details. I've got a larger point to make. The stretches between our face-to-face visits can get hard, but like so many other separated loved ones, Jessica and I have developed ways to be a part of each other's daily lives. We e-mail, we text, and of course, we use the phone. Sometimes we don't have much phone time or we don't have that much to say, but we still want the contact. For those occasions we've developed something called "That's all I've got."

Jessica will call and say, "I just saw the funniest billboard." Or maybe she'll say, "Grant just did the funniest thing." Regardless of what prompted the call, she'll describe a small segment of her day, I'll comment, and then she'll say, "That's all I've got." In our relationship that means, "I just wanted to hear your voice." We sign off a bit happier and a little more content in spite of our separation.

> Just as our interactions with God aren't meant to be restricted to a devotional time, neither should they be reserved for times of crisis or the need to rant.

Our conversations with God can work in much the same way. Not every prayer has to be long on detail and passion; sometimes a quick word with Him provides just the connection we're craving during the day. True, we'll never grow closer to the Lord by shooting up haphazard little phrases if we aren't also looking to spend quality time with Him. That said, incorporating some "that's all I've got" moments during the day will make those fall-down-on-our-knees prayers all the more precious, simply because we are choosing to nurture this divine friendship. It's about an ongoing relationship. God wants it. We need it. Let's do it.

DAY BY DAY

I hope I've whetted your appetite for seeking God all through the day instead of only at a set time. I hope you'll begin taking those middle-of-the-day frustrations to God rather than to others, and I hope you'll begin to "use your words" and practice "That's all I've got" moments, because I know they'll pay great dividends in your faith. And should you get sidetracked or distracted midprayer or find your faith flagging at any time, day or night, I hope you'll take a pass on the guilt and just run home to Jesus anyway.

As I type these words, the birds in my backyard are singing at the tops of their little voices. Life is one big all-you-can-eat buffet for this particular avian population. Every day I fill up their bird feeder. Every day they empty it. Apparently, good news travels fast, even in Bird Land. And yet, at the risk of overstating the obvious, my backyard birds are so, well, flighty. They are ridiculously tentative about gathering at my feeder. Although it supplied their needs yesterday, they return today cautiously, one by one, like nervous, suspicious little addicts, not entirely sure they'll find what they seek. And heaven forbid the wind chimes stir or a leaf blows nearby. The slightest movement or sound results in a mass exodus from the feeder as they abandon their nourishment. Hello, Jane Sparrow, I'm talking to you—and to me!

Day by day the Lord faithfully offers us His sweet presence and provision. Sometimes we manage to feed on His Word and rest in His care, but too often the first hint of trouble frightens us or something shiny catches our eyes and off we go, scurrying away from our Source when we should be hurrying to Him!

Let's determine not to trade the best this life has to offer for the stirring of the wind. Instead, when we find ourselves distracted, as we inevitably will, let's simply turn around and head home.

Dear Lord, I've been guilty of trying to find time for You in my days, but it has been a hit-and-miss experience at best. I want to find You in my days instead! I want to learn to live in awareness of You and with my heart turned toward You. Help me be quick to notice when I've become distracted by the cares of this world, and help me be quick to run home. Amen.

5

ARE SOME OF US STUCK WITH
MESSED-UP MUSTARD SEEDS?

"Lord, I want to grow in my faith.
Show me what's holding me back."

*W*oo-hoo! I've been looking forward to this next discussion since page 1, and yet I'm tempted even now to back into this chapter on obedience or ease into it ever so gently. Generally speaking, obedience is not a subject that fills auditoriums or sells books, but if we understood the rewards of choosing God's ways over our own, it would be!

Do you remember the first time you fell in love? Do you remember trying to think of ways to show your sweetheart that you loved him? Obedience can bring us to such a place with Jesus, a place where we see bending our will to His as an opportunity to demonstrate our love to Him. We can come to see that moment of submission not as something we have to do, but as something we get to do as a gift of our devotion. In practical terms it means we can offer someone grace instead of that tempting tongue lashing. Through obedience, we can offer that flesh-and-blood person grace because we are offering it as a gift to our supernatural God for the amazing grace He continues to pour out on us!

That's why, instead of making excuses or disclaimers about what follows, I want to make you a promise: if you hang in with me, I'll show you the blessing of obeying God and how bending our will to His acts like Miracle-Gro for our mustard seeds! So if you really want to make your way through this life in conversation with the God you believe in, stick around. If you're serious about knowing Him intimately and cranking up your faith, lean in.

When things are largely okay in our world and we feel like we can handle our everyday problems, even if we're rather worn down by the daily demands and frustrations of life, it's easy to become complacent about our mediocre or stagnant faith. This false sense of security lulls us into a dangerous place of accepting the distance we feel from God. We may realize we're not in the same league as Moses, Elijah, or the great apostle Paul, and for the most part, we're okay with that. We may even have a nagging sense that there is more to faith than we're experiencing, but we can usually rationalize the problem away by convincing ourselves that we're just being realistic about our expectations.

> ### If you're serious about knowing Him intimately, lean in.

It's those other days—the ones that bring a scary doctor's report, rebellious kids, job loss, death, and natural tragedy—that come at us like a spiritual strip search. Our faith feels naked and exposed. Suddenly, we need to hear God and we need to know God hears us. Shaken and challenged, we cry out for more. Southerners call this moment of crisis a "Come to Jesus meeting," and it's exactly where we find Jesus's right-hand men in Luke 17. Jesus was talking to His disciples about sin, faith, and our duty to forgive when He said,

Things that cause people to sin are bound to come, but woe to that person through whom they come. It would be better for him to be thrown into the sea with a millstone tied around his neck than for him to cause one of these little ones to sin. So watch yourselves.

If your brother sins, rebuke him, and if he repents, forgive him. If he sins against you seven times in a day, and seven times comes back to you and says, "I repent," forgive him. (verses 1–4, NIV)

The disciples' response sounds a lot like the prayer that opens our chapter. The men seemed to be taken aback by Jesus asking them to practice what they considered an unusual amount of forgiveness. In the face of such a strong challenge, the Twelve eyeballed each other, looked back at Jesus, and responded with something equivalent to "Houston, we have a problem."

The apostles said to the Lord, "Increase our faith!" (verse 5).

Good for them. The disciples were rattled, but at least they knew where to go in an emergency: 911–JESUS!

That being said, does their distress call strike you as being a tad off target? When told to practice what looks to us like extreme forgiveness, the guys asked for more faith. Doesn't it seem like they should have asked for more patience instead?

Let's consider the problem from our own experience. To forgive someone five, six, even seven times for the same offense requires a lot from us, doesn't it? We have to deny our tendency to keep score. Could it be that the idea of demonstrating such extravagant forgiveness left the disciples comparing their lives with the way Jesus was asking them to live and discovering that their faith was woefully ill-equipped for the challenge? Perhaps that's why they decided they needed a bigger, stronger faith. Let's see how Jesus responded.

Wow, Jesus! Tell Us How You Really Feel

Verse 6 explodes with what I fondly call The Big Faith Advertisement. In it, Jesus made a famous claim about a tiny mustard seed that continues to rock our world more than two thousand years later. In response to the disciples' request for more faith, Jesus said, "If you have faith as small as a mustard seed, you can say to this mulberry tree, 'Be uprooted and planted in the sea,' and it will obey you."

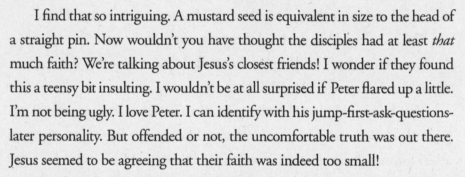

God always desires to conceive in us a bigger vision than the one we're imagining.

I find that so intriguing. A mustard seed is equivalent in size to the head of a straight pin. Now wouldn't you have thought the disciples had at least *that* much faith? We're talking about Jesus's closest friends! I wonder if they found this a teensy bit insulting. I wouldn't be at all surprised if Peter flared up a little. I'm not being ugly. I love Peter. I can identify with his jump-first-ask-questions-later personality. But offended or not, the uncomfortable truth was out there. Jesus seemed to be agreeing that their faith was indeed too small!

You do realize that the disciples hadn't asked for a mulberry-tree-growing-in-the-sea type of faith, right? They had asked only for enough faith to practice forgiveness in a bigger way. I find Jesus's answer to be beautifully characteristic. God always desires to conceive in us a bigger vision than the one we're imagining!

Jesus responded to their request for more faith with a declaration of the amazing things they could see if they were to operate in even the most minimal amount of faith. If you'll allow me some creative license, I hear Jesus saying something like this: "I'm glad you're asking for stronger faith, guys, because frankly, the faith you're operating in right now doesn't even come close to what my Father and I can make available to you!"

Well, would you look at this? In essence, Jesus was egging 'em on! He was challenging His followers (that includes us) to grasp an enormous truth: extreme forgiveness is entirely possible—along with a whole array of other incredible feats—for the one who lives by faith.

We aren't privy to what the Big Twelve thought or said about this divine answer, but I'm afraid my response might have sounded like, "Uh, yes sir. That sounds great, sir! That's exactly the type of faith I need, sir. But, with all due respect, sir, I was asking You to give it to me!" (I'd toss in all those *sirs* to make sure I didn't sound lippy. That's Mama's word. When I was growing up, being lippy could get me in hot water faster than quick.)

For the disciples and those of us listening in, the big question is still on the table; Jesus has only broadened it. How can we cultivate a faith that not only forgives to the extreme but also produces mulberry-tree-growing-in-the-sea type of results? If you're holding your breath for the answer, you're in good company. Check out the expression on the disciples' faces. You don't need an overactive imagination like mine to picture them leaning forward, hanging on Jesus's next words, which to my mind take a curious turn:

> Suppose one of you had a servant plowing or looking after the sheep.
> Would he say to the servant when he comes in from the field, "Come
> along now and sit down to eat"? Would he not rather say, "Prepare my
> supper, get yourself ready and wait on me while I eat and drink; after
> that you may eat and drink"? Would he thank the servant because he
> did what he was told to do? So you also, when you have done every-
> thing you were told to do, should say, "We are unworthy servants; we
> have only done our duty." (Luke 17:7–10, NIV)

Did we miss something? After proclaiming the potent possibilities of faith, Jesus abruptly moved into a discussion of a man and his servant that seems entirely off topic. But is it? Cue the mystery music. *Da-da-da-dummmm!*

What if Jesus hadn't changed subjects at all? What if He was laying out the how-to for developing a faith that could uproot both mulberry trees and bitterness in a single bound? There's obviously something more going on here than we see at first glance, so let's keep looking.

WHO'S THE BOSS?

The servant analogy probably resonated more clearly for the disciples than it does for us twenty-first-century believers. So before we drill down any further, we need to establish a foundational truth about our true position in the kingdom.

First Corinthians 6:19–20 tells it straight: "Do you not know that your body is a temple of the Holy Spirit who is in you, whom you have from God, and that you are not your own? For you have been bought with a price: therefore glorify God in your body."

"You are not your own." That's not a comfortable idea for those of us raised in a culture where "You're not the boss of me" seems to be the driving theme, but if we are to grow in our faith, we absolutely must surrender our bluster and acknowledge that Jesus is not only our Savior. He is our Master.

This desire to be lord of our own universe may be dormant at birth, but it all too quickly shows up and takes charge. For Exhibit A, I offer you the Toddler's Rules of Possession:

1. If I like it, it's mine.
2. If it's in my hand, it's mine.
3. If I can take it from you, it's mine.

4. If I had it a little while ago, it's mine.

5. If it's mine, it must NEVER appear to be yours in any way.

6. If I'm doing or building something, all the pieces are mine.

7. If it looks just like mine, it is mine.

8. If I saw it first, it's mine.

9. If you are playing with something and you put it down, it automatically becomes mine.

10. If it's broken, it's yours.

Oh, and that's just the beginning! During our formative years we chafe at the rules of our parents, teachers, and coaches. Then we join the adult world, where we find ourselves straining just as hard against a host of other self-appointed rulers, each wanting to dictate all manner of things in our lives. Digging in our heels becomes a reflexive action. Of course resistance isn't always a bad thing. Some people don't deserve to wield authority. They thrive on manipulating others. But I'm not talking about capitulating to control freaks, and I'm not talking about the proper response to a boss in the workplace, either. Dealing with those interpersonal relationships would require another conversation entirely. I'm challenging us to fully adopt the only correct response to the greatest Authority on earth, to bow low and profess, "You are God and I am not."

As we read in 1 Chronicles 16:31, "Let the heavens be glad, and let the earth rejoice; and let them say among the nations, 'The LORD reigns.'" No greater authority exists in heaven or on earth, and yet He gives us the freedom to choose whether or not we'll submit our will to His. This decision ever lies before us, and the right choice carries a treasure we often are slow to see.

Underline this, circle it, or tweet it: Anything God requires of us is for our benefit. He doesn't demand obedience simply to say, "Me, God—you, servant." Obedience is for us, so that by aligning ourselves with His purposes we can enjoy the great unearned gift of His abiding presence. When we yield our wills to God's, the question of "What's in it for me?" is answered with a resounding, "Everything!"

When Jesus instructed His disciples to follow His example, He said, "Now that you know these things, you will be blessed if you do them" (John 13:17, NIV).

Before we're done with this chapter, we'll spend some more time in John's gospel to explore just how that happens. Right now, let's get back to the scene in Luke where the Twelve were wondering where to find this amazing mustard-seed faith Jesus had described.

I believe Jesus used the disciples' understanding of the master-slave relationship to illustrate a life-transforming truth: Ever-increasing faith is available to us, but it's not a "you asked for it, you got it" proposition. Our faith grows through submitting our wills and our agendas to God the way the servant in Jesus's story yielded his will to the master's.

Jesus wanted His followers to know that they already had the necessary faith to forgive again and again; they just needed to learn to obey. We might feel more like celebrating if that didn't leave us right back there at square one, right? Like us, the disciples couldn't see past their current reality to imagine living as He described. Ever-increasing faith to obey looks like the impossible dream, given what we know to be true of our uninspiring spiritual experience to date. What gives? What's wrong with our mustard seed?

Absolutely nothing.

IT'S THE WILL THAT GETS IN THE WAY

Be encouraged. Your mustard seed is fine. It's not subpar to your saintly pastor's or your Jesus-loving neighbor's. Not only can you learn to obey, you have already begun to obey or you wouldn't even have that precious mustard seed of faith that bids you to press on to know Him more intimately!

The very first step of obedience we ever take is to agree with what God says about us, that we are lost and we are powerless to save ourselves. Believing in Jesus and trusting in salvation through faith is our obedient response to His finished work on the cross. We lay down our lives to receive His. In the same way, the deepening friendship and growing faith we crave is directly tied to continuing to give up our right to ourselves.

Ongoing, present-tense submission exercises our faith muscles. This was Jesus's message on obedience. He tied ever-increasing faith to the disciples exercising the faith that was already theirs.

Don't let that word *exercise* worry you. We're not going to the gym. But likening the fuzzy concept of exercising our faith to the very concrete practice of exercising our bodies can help us grasp this important truth. By definition, to exercise is to "subject to practice or exertion in order to train, strengthen, or develop."[4] It involves the regular or repeated use of a faculty or muscle. Exercise is a drill carried out for training and discipline that engages the attention and effort of the muscle. In its simplest form, exercise is resistance to an opposing weight or force.

We all know *how* to exercise our bodies. I think I speak for most of us when I say it's the *will* that gets in the way. Do I hear an amen? I can dress in my warmup suit, tennis shoes, and headband. I can pin my intentions on Pinterest. I can study carefully everything there is to know about exercise. I can stand in the exercise room for years and even hold a weight in my hand every morning for a certain length of time, but the brutal truth is that my muscles will not grow if I don't move the weight.

Likewise, we can study the Word, quote the Word, and speak the Word. We can sit and stand in church year after year. We can have amazing head knowledge about the Bible. But until we submit our own desires to God's and apply resistance to the "weight" of our flesh, our faith won't grow. Our pastors are called to shepherd God's people here on earth, but they can't guarantee our personal growth any more than you can lift weights to make my biceps grow. Only our own personal resistance training—regularly moving aside the weight of our flesh to choose God's will over our own—leads to increased faith.

Are you thinking that I have totally lost sight of the problem here, that I've somehow forgotten how incapable we are of sticking to God's workout plan? I assure you that I haven't. As a matter of fact, I'm getting giddy just thinking about the good news I'm about to type out on this keyboard: Girlfriend, the One who lives *in* us has accomplished *for* us what God the Father knew we never could.

> For what the Law could not do, weak as it was through the flesh, God
> did: sending His own Son in the likeness of sinful flesh and as an
> offering for sin, He condemned sin in the flesh, so that the require-
> ment of the Law might be fulfilled in us, who do not walk according
> to the flesh but according to the Spirit. (Romans 8:3–4)

Remember when we talked about the Holy Spirit living in us to give us the courage to keep following Jesus into the great unknown? The blessed Spirit of the living Christ also indwells in us as the Supreme Personal Trainer. He has an unblemished record of submission to God's plan, and He dwells in us that we might profit from His finished work. Our part is to embrace this gift and realize that the only way we can obey God is to continually draw from His victory instead of falling back into the trap of struggling to achieve our own.

Without a doubt, yielding our will to God's can be very difficult. The flesh gets loud about demanding its way. But when we submit and choose humility—exalting the Father's will over our own—we're empowered to obey through the grace of the One who lives in us. First Peter reminds us, "God resists the proud, but gives grace to the humble" (5:5, NKJV).

Christ lives *in* us to obey *for* us. That's shouting news. Colossians 1:27 declares the marvelous riches of this truth as "Christ in you, the hope of glory."

> When we choose to obey,
> God's grace empowers our decision.

The gospel is so much more glorious than the message we have often presented. That Jesus died on the cross to forgive us of our sins and give us eternal life is good news indeed, but without the rest of the story we would be orphans, and Jesus promised us that this would not be the case: "I will not leave you as orphans; I will come to you. After a little while the world will no longer see Me, but you will see Me" (John 14:18–19).

The Holy Spirit lives in us as a guarantee of the promise to come. He is our ever-present help. Every day brings us countless tailor-made moments to rely on Him, to experience that rock-solid promise for ourselves and see our faith increase.

Many times these opportunities to bend our will in obedience to His are presented through other people. If you've ever been hurt repeatedly by the same person, you know that the temptation to count how many times you've forgiven is always there. Speaking for myself, I know what I should do, but sometimes I'd rather wallow in self-pity, defend myself in a one-way conversation in my head, or take my case to the other party and demand answers for what I see as unfair treatment. I confess, sometimes I'm not as quick to choose His way as I should be, but He has taught me the value of bringing my frustration and pain to Him in unvarnished honesty.

I'll tell Him that I'm hurt and that I don't feel like forgiving again. *(How many times do You expect me to do this, Lord? I'm pretty sure we passed seven awhile back!)* I may even rant openly to Him about how this is wrong and I'm being treated unfairly. And then, even as I am dumping my ugly emotions on

Him, God begins to love on me. He gently reminds me of the forgiveness He prepared for me when I was far from Him and wanted none of it. He softens my heart until I do want to reach out again to the one who has hurt me. He points out that the real issue is the pain buried in the person's heart and urges me not to join with the Enemy by contributing to it. The world around me may not have seen the miracle. No one else may know the revengeful plots my soul first conceived or witness the wide swing between my initial reaction and my response after being transformed by an infusion of His power once I yielded to His way. But I see it and my heart bears witness: this is none other than the mysterious enabling grace of Jesus Christ.

When I forgive an offense (or what I see as an offense), when I choose thankfulness when I feel like complaining, when I deny myself the right to choose my own response to a situation, however large or small, I'm exercising my faith. I'm saying in essence, "I'm not my own master. I'm subject to what I can't see. I've been bought with a price, and I must choose my Savior's will over my own!"

But the opposite is equally true. When I'm determined to do what I want to do when I want to do it, and I give myself permission, I'm choosing disobedience and forfeiting the unequaled pleasure of His presence and His life in me.

The problem most often is not that we set out to place our rebellious wills over His but that we put what we consider to be innocent excuses on the moments when we choose personal lordship. It bears saying outright: Our adversary, the devil, wants us to believe we have a choice as to whether or not we'll live and walk in obedience. We don't—not if we want to live a victorious Christian life, not if we want mulberry-tree-growing-in-the-sea faith. If we want our mustard seed to flourish, we must choose to obey.

Much as we may want others to see Christ in us, they won't until *we* see Christ in us! The challenge is to recognize the everyday moments that present us with an opportunity to choose His way or our own.

This Is That Moment

I used to think it would be great if someone would hold up a flashing sign and activate a siren whenever I'm being given the chance to exercise my faith. The sign could read, THIS IS THAT MOMENT! and I would snap to attention and realize just what's at stake in the pause between knowing the right thing and doing it. But it's not going to happen, and I've come to realize what a blessing that is! When Jesus arose and returned to heaven, He made a way for us to experience something far greater. Through the gift of the Holy Spirit, we have the privilege of *choosing to listen for God's inside voice*!

Jesus said, "But I tell you the truth, it is to your advantage that I go away; for if I do not go away, the Helper will not come to you; but if I go, I will send Him to you.... When He, the Spirit of truth, comes, He will guide you into all the truth" (John 16:7, 13).

I can't follow you around with a flashing "THIS IS THAT MOMENT!" sign, and you wouldn't want me to. But if you ask the Holy Spirit to help you become more aware of these moments, He will be faithful to do so, and you'll become addicted to the pressure of His hand on your heart.

I want to be as clear here as I possibly can. Placing your faith in the blood of Jesus Christ is what saves you. That's the unmerited favor of God. Ephesians 2:8–9 reads, "For by grace you have been saved through faith; and that not of yourselves, it is the gift of God; not as a result of works, so that no one may boast."

Obedience doesn't save us from our sins; it accesses and ignites what faith has already received. It is God's grace that sustains us, and it is His grace that will one day take us to live with Him for all eternity. How fully we live in Him here before we arrive there lies with us. Obedience does not secure our salvation, but without it we will never know the unparalleled joy and security of walking with Him on this side of heaven.

Oh, that we would continually submit and rely on His ever-loving grace! Ask for grace to obey. Depend on grace to obey, and thrill in the grace He gives us to obey, for it is the secret of great joy. The greatest blessing of obedience is the consciousness of His presence. King David celebrated it this way: "The LORD is my portion; I have promised to keep Your words" (Psalm 119:57, HCSB).

Truly, the reward of obeying God is to personally experience Him. Hear the beautiful words God spoke to Abraham: "After this, the word of the LORD came to Abram in a vision: 'Do not be afraid, Abram. I am your shield, your very great reward'" (Genesis 15:1, NIV).

I hope you're feeling this thing! When we yield our will to God's, He draws near to work out through us the faith He has placed within us. Second Chronicles 16:9 paints yet another beautiful picture of God's response to our submission: "For the eyes of the LORD run to and fro throughout the whole earth, to show Himself strong on behalf of those whose heart is loyal to Him" (NKJV).

Oh, do you see Him? Use that wonderful imagination He gave you and picture Him leaning over heaven's balcony, looking, scanning, searching, to show Himself strong on behalf of an obedient servant. "Ah, there she is," He says to Gabriel, or maybe it's Michael standing there. "There she is, choosing to obey me. Do you see her, mighty angel? Isn't she a treasure? I will show Myself strong in her life, for this one is loyal to Me!"

Tell me, if God showed His strength on your behalf, would your faith not increase? So, according to the scriptures we just read, what moves God? Obedience! And we're equipped to be obedient by the grace of Christ at work in us, empowering us to choose His ways. It is a beautiful circle of blessing. When we obey God, our faith grows. When our faith grows, we're increasingly motivated to obey Him. Our faith—what Hebrews 11:1 defines as "the assurance of things hoped for, the conviction of things not seen"—matures when we begin to experience God in the moments of our daily lives.

The Lord Jesus spelled out the beautiful truth in a clear and heartening promise: "Whoever has my commands and obeys them, he is the one who loves me. He who loves me will be loved by my Father, and I too will love him and show myself to him" (John 14:21, NIV). There's Jesus, promising to abide in close fellowship with the one who walks in obedience. Talk about a faith builder!

> **Obedience is our greatest expression of love for God.**

In the event you aren't shouting yet, here's the same passage in the Amplified version: "The person who has My commands and keeps them is the one who [really] loves Me; and whoever [really] loves Me will be loved by My Father, and I [too] will love him and will show (reveal, manifest) Myself to him. [I will let Myself be clearly seen by him and make Myself real to him.]"

Will you savor that with me? The same God who calls the stars out by name and tells the ocean how far it can roam (see Isaiah 40:26; Job 38:11) will reveal Himself, manifest Himself, and let Himself be clearly seen by the one who obeys Him. I may need a moment.

Do you want a more vibrant, exuberant, irrepressible faith, a life-shaping friendship with God that will strengthen you for extreme forgiveness and so much more? Submit to God and He will show Himself to you by showing Himself in you. The surest sign *to* you of this almighty God *in* you will be your changing desires. Day by day His friendship will transform your heart and increase your faith.

Someone recently stopped me in my busy little tracks to launch into what looked to be a long conversation. I was feeling anxious about a host of other things I needed to be doing, but I knew the person in front of me needed me to hear him out. I could feel my impatience warring with the Word in me, "Each of you should look not only to your own interests, but also to the interests of others" (Philippians 2:4, NIV). As soon as I chose to put my agenda aside and really listen, I felt God's pleasure.

Girlfriend, you can know God's pleasure too. To obey Him is to abide in Him—to find your life and purpose in Him—and that experience is unequalled.

We often think of obedience in terms of obeying the written Word of God, and that is certainly part of it. But Jesus, the living Word, is always speaking to us, always calling us to another way of thinking, another way of speaking, truly another way of living. He came into the world to show us the Truth, God in human form. To experience Him we must bend our will to His, but such surrender will set us free, and free indeed. Life's greatest ongoing adventure is walking, talking, and abiding with the Creator.

The entire New Testament, the gospel, the good news—it's all about this new way, this inner obedience, the transformation of our entire selves that happens when we yield our will to His. Think of obedience as a way of living instead of acts of doing, and you'll soon be saying with the psalmist, "I run in the path of your commands, for you have set my heart free" (119:32, NIV). This is the blessing of obeying God. Pleasing Him becomes our delight. Instead of trying to live right so God will walk and talk with us, we begin to understand that when we walk and talk with Him, we will live right.

COME ONE, COME ALL

In our opening passage from Luke, Jesus told His disciples to practice unlimited forgiveness, and they asked for more faith to do it. Instead of granting them increased faith, Jesus explained that the problem was one of obedience. I believe He's saying the same thing to us today, and not just to a chosen few. This opportunity isn't rarified air for the privileged or superblessed, the pastor and the church staff, or the Type-A personalities. We were born for this kind of living.

In John 10:10 Jesus was speaking of all His sheep when He said, "I have come that they may have life, and that they may have it more abundantly" (NKJV). Jesus calls us to obedience because He knows it is what's best for us.

I remember looking down into the earnest eyes of my disobedient first grandchild. "It's okay, Keggie," Emerson said to me. "I didn't mean to!"

It was hard to maintain a stern gaze as I looked into her sweet-as-sugar upturned face. Emerson Ann was supposed to be taking her afternoon nap—or trying to, anyway. Her mother's rules were clear. Even if she couldn't fall asleep, Emerson was supposed to stay in bed and quietly look at her picture books. The dear child, however, was neither sleeping nor resting. What's more, she had gotten out of bed to diaper her stuffed bear in the next room and accidentally slammed the bedroom door, waking up her sleeping baby sister, who was now crying from her crib.

My scolding had brought us to this moment. "It's okay, Keggie," Emerson repeated. "I didn't mean to!" Clearly, she was hoping this would make it all better in a "Let's just forget this and go watch *Mickey Mouse Clubhouse*" sort of way. Of course, you and I both see the problem, right? The result of her actions may have been an accident, but the disobedience that led to it was all too intentional.

Emerson was pushing three at the time, and while her infraction wasn't that serious, I was happy to reinforce the message her parents had been giving as they confronted their daughter's favorite new excuse with age-appropriate logic and discipline. I concurred with them for all the usual reasons, but here's the most important one: If Emerson is to grow up to enjoy a healthy relationship with Christ, learning obedience is crucial. She won't obey Him if she never learns to submit to authority.

Willful disobedience before God, however small, will always lead to broken fellowship, but those who learn to yield to His Lordship and readily bend their wills to His get to discover the sweet reward of His friendship. It's an all-important life lesson that can't begin too soon. God doesn't require anything of us just for His divine kicks! His commandments are always for our own good. Your obedience will never make God any more God than He already is, but your submission *will* reveal more of His glory in your life.

For sure, Emerson was cute as a bug standing there with a big smile on her face, but I called her hand, precisely because she has my heart.

He Longs to Call Us Friends

We opened this chapter with a discussion of a dutiful servant in Luke 17. Jesus noted that the Master expects the servant to put his own desires last—and that the servant shouldn't anticipate any thanks or praise for doing so. Perhaps you've been wondering how to reconcile the idea of being Christ's servant with being His friend. The wonderful truth is that divine friendship with Jesus isn't at odds with His expectation of our obedience. Jesus said,

> You are my friends if you do what I command. I no longer call you
> servants, because a servant does not know his master's business.
> Instead, I have called you friends, for everything that I learned from
> my Father I have made known to you. You did not choose me, but I
> chose you and appointed you to go and bear fruit—fruit that will last.
> (John 15:14–16, NIV)

When does Jesus call us friends? Exactly! He calls us friends when we do what He commands. I want to be a good friend to the best Friend that I have ever found, the Friend who sticks closer than a brother.

Down through the ages, certain men and women have shaken the earth with their faith. I will dare to say that all these believers learned obedience. Let's join them.

Remember the persuasive words of the old hymn:

Trust and obey,
For there's no other way
To be happy in Jesus,
But to trust and obey.[5]

There's nothing wrong with your mustard seed. The issue is not how much faith you have at this moment but what you're going to do with what you've been given. No one gets a head start or a bad draw, and nothing can stand in the way of anyone who decides to deny his or her own self and run after Jesus.

How about it? Are you ready? On your mark, get set, *go!*

Lord, I want a stronger faith. Help me love Your ways and submit to Your Word. Help me recognize when an opportunity is before me to choose Your will over my own, and remind me in that moment that You live in me to empower me to obey. I want to walk in obedience so that I can know the increasing joy of abiding in You and having You abide in me. Amen.

6

WE ARE ALWAYS ON OUR MIND

"I'm having trouble keeping my eyes off me and on You, Lord. Help!"

I was born with a beat in my feet. Honestly, I have a difficult time understanding people who don't feel a similar rhythm in their own shoes. By people, I really mean one person in particular. I've been married to the love of my life for more than three decades, and not once have I seen my man lose himself to a beat. Fast beats or slow beats, Phil is genetically immune to them all. I, on the other hand, can dance to the washing machine when it gets out of balance.

We used to see ourselves in a commercial that opened with a couple sitting on a park bench. Well, to be accurate, the man was sitting on the bench, completely motionless and absorbed in his newspaper. His sweetie, meanwhile, was doing everything but sitting. She danced, skipped, and jived all around that bench to the sound of nothing, or so it seemed. I get that.

Wasn't it Thoreau who first said, "If a man does not keep pace with his companions, perhaps it is because he hears a different drummer"?[6] I would add that some of us can tap out a beat in our heads even if we don't hear one in our ears. Others, well, their lives seem to flow without benefit of a beat of any kind, like my tempo-bereft man.

Poor Phil. I've been known to study my guy as if he were a science experiment to see if any part of him is responding to the praise music blaring from our car's speakers. "Tell the truth, honey. Are you at least moving a toe inside your boot?"

We frustrate the grace of Christ Jesus by micromanaging our faith.

My darling inevitably responds with a grin and a denial. "Nope, sorry."

Phil and I have come to a truce about our dancing differences. We never go out just to go dancing, but he will slow dance with me at wedding receptions, emphasis on slow. If we were moving any slower, birds would build nests in our hair, but hey—we're dancing and I love him for it! I suppose it goes without saying that my man passed up the invitation to take ballroom-dance lessons with me. I watched from afar as that craze swept the nation. So to set up the analogy I have in mind for this chapter, I'll borrow the experience of two of my friends.

Becky told me that she and her husband, Greg, loved their ballroom-dancing lessons, but she had the hardest time learning not to lead. Her teacher constantly reminded her to give in and follow Greg, but try as she might, Becky couldn't refrain from directing the process. Of course, this frustrated their progress for quite some time. Only after Becky learned to place herself in Greg's hands and *keep her eyes closed* was the couple able to enjoy the experience. And that, my friend, is a good snapshot of the predicament we can find ourselves in even after we determine to give ourselves over to heaven's precious beat. If we aren't careful, we'll frustrate the grace of Christ Jesus by micromanaging our faith.

Sadly, if we try to follow the path Jesus blazed by focusing on our own feet, we will get tripped up every single time. With that in mind, there's someone I need you to meet while we're still digesting that last chapter on the link between obeying God and knowing Him more intimately.

THE EVIL TWIN

Meet Legalism, the evil twin of Obedience. She is crafty, subtle, and highly adaptable. Legalism knows how to slip out of one disguise and into another to blend in with the times. She's a longtime foe of genuine faith—and still she manages to slither around undetected, masquerading as Virtue. I hinted at her evil ways in an earlier chapter when I promised we'd take a closer look at "performance religion." Now we're about to take that look—at her wiles and her weak spots. Legalism may be good at her game because she's been at it for ages, but expose her to the blood of Jesus and she loses every single time.

The apostle Paul had zero patience for legalism. He was adamant about the importance of our obedience to Christ, but he was careful to teach that it was based on love flowing from a grateful heart. Consider his words to the church at Colossae: "So then, just as you received Christ Jesus as Lord, continue to live in him, rooted and built up in him, strengthened in the faith as you were taught, and overflowing with thankfulness" (Colossians 2:6–7, NIV).

We received Christ freely by grace through faith. We learn to walk in Him and grow in Him the same way. Had Paul not relied on Christ for strength and patience, the good apostle may have burned out preaching this message to listeners who couldn't seem to rest in the finished work of the Cross. The temptation for Paul's audience was to combine a dash of grace with a generous measure of Old Testament Law until they achieved a confidence born not of faith in Christ, *but of their own efforts to obey Him.*

That's Legalism impersonating Obedience, and Paul blew her cover in the first few verses of Galatians 3:

You foolish Galatians! Who has hypnotized you, before whose eyes
Jesus Christ was vividly portrayed as crucified? I only want to learn this
from you: Did you receive the Spirit by the works of the law or by
hearing with faith? Are you so foolish? After beginning with the Spirit,
are you now going to be made complete by the flesh? (verses 1–3, HCSB)

That Paul! I don't know why he holds back.

But seriously, we might be tempted to skim over this strong language,
satisfied that we don't have much, if anything, in common with the folks
Paul was dressing down here. I mean, I'm not longing for the Old Testament
Law. Are you? But it's dangerously naive of us to conclude that we're exempt
from Paul's warning. We can be deceived just as easily as our predecessors
into "beginning with the Spirit" and then trying "to be made complete by
the flesh."

The only thing works-based religion will ever give us is a bone-dry, guilt-
ridden experience. Legalism's evil goal is to keep us from God. Legalism's evil
method is to keep us so focused on trying to do more for Him that we lose
focus on what He has already done in Christ for us.

Satan never quits trying to come between God and His people. Just as he
deceives and harasses those who don't know God to dissuade them from
coming to Him through Christ, the Enemy is always working to keep believers from enjoying the full benefits of their relationship in Christ.

Jesus fulfilled the Law. Satan knows we're no longer bound by it, but
bondage is his specialty, and he never stops trying to get us to adopt our own
homemade laws to try and keep us from knowing our God. But note what
Paul told the believers in Colossians 2. After instructing them on how to
walk out their faith in verses 6 and 7, he warned them, "See to it that no one
takes you captive through hollow and deceptive philosophy, which depends

on human tradition and the basic principles of this world rather than on Christ" (verse 8, NIV).

"See to it that *no one* takes you captive." It was a long time before I realized that I could take my own self captive. What's more, I was quite good at it! I knew that the Bible says to be angry and sin not. So if I lost my temper, I had missed the mark. I couldn't simply agree with God that my behavior was wrong, ask for forgiveness, and follow on after Jesus if I still *felt* guilty. If I sensed distance in my relationship with God, I would try to confess with enough sincere remorse to warrant His forgiveness and to *feel* forgiven. Not only was that a hopeless cause, but with every effort at earning His favor, my homemade chains only tightened around my feet. Oh, the deception! It took me a long time to recognize Legalism for the imposter that she is. I'd been aware since childhood that the Enemy will try to tempt me with what is wrong, but I was much slower to understand that he is eager to use my very desire to live in Christ against me.

It is not repenting for the sake of repenting that grants me access to God. It is trusting in the finished work of the Cross.

I have no desire to sin, but now, when I fall short, I acknowledge it to the Father, and I rest in Jesus who is my righteousness, "who has been tempted in all things as we are, yet without sin" (Hebrews 4:15). I do not judge my standing with God according to whether or not I feel that our relationship is restored. The Enemy wants us to establish our own measures of righteousness so that we never learn to live fully in Christ Jesus who is "our righteousness, holiness and redemption" (1 Corinthians 1:30, NIV), but my confidence is in nothing but the atoning blood of Christ.

This believer has spent far too much time entangled in laws of my own making. Beyond my salvation, one of the things I most frequently thank God for is freeing me from me.

THE BLESSING OF LIVING FREE FROM ME

After urging his listeners to be careful that no one took them captive, Paul spent a few moments explaining what those chains might look like. He talked about religious feast days and ordinances, about not touching this or touching that—all traditions held over from the Levitical laws of their past. For us, these traps might look like attending church because it's expected of us, giving to missions out of a sense of guilt, or filling in all the blanks of our Bible study. Or it may look like those check-off devotionals we talked about earlier. But hear what Paul said about all such attempts to grab hold of Good Girl status: "Which things have indeed a show of wisdom in will-worship, and humility, and severity to the body; but are not of any value against the indulgence of the flesh" (Colossians 2:23, ASV).

Serving God isn't a self-improvement course we follow out of sheer determination, for such efforts "are not of any value against the indulgence of the flesh." No value? My gut-it-out efforts to please Him apart from depending on His grace are of no value? Ouch, again.

Showy acts of self-denial and self-rule, whether offered to obey my own laws or impress others, accomplish nothing! Obedience born of love and dependent on Christ will strengthen my faith, but my flesh will win every single time if I'm trying to deny it in my own power.

> Serving God is not a self-improvement course
> we follow out of sheer determination.

Do-it-myself righteousness is just another way to worship my will. It satisfies the flesh while grieving God. When I try to feel better about myself apart from the perfect and complete sacrifice of His Son, I'm basically saying that what Jesus did wasn't enough. That one thought makes me determined to run from the first hint of legalism!

Oh yes, you're looking at a reformed will worshiper. But as surely as the recovering alcoholic understands that he or she is forever susceptible to falling off the wagon, I know that if I take my eyes off the finished work of the Cross, history is bound to repeat itself. Truly, the only way to keep my feet untangled from my self-made laws is to live in constant awareness that this abundant and ever-increasing life in Christ is mine through Him and His blood alone.

The apostle Paul warned us about Legalism's tactic of cloaking itself in outward goodness.

> And this commandment, which was to result in life, proved to result in death for me; for sin, taking an opportunity through the commandment, deceived me and through it killed me. So then, the Law is holy, and the commandment is holy and righteous and good. (Romans 7:10–12)

Paul taught that the Law was given to show us our sin and our hopelessness apart from grace by revealing God's holy character and how far we fall short of it. And yet, Paul said, sin used that revelation of God's holiness to agitate him and increase its presence in his life by making him more aware of his failures than ever! News flash: sin still seeks to do this. Right now, this moment, today, sin seeks to gain power through the revelation of how far we fall short of God's standard. Surely you've noticed that the Enemy seizes every opportunity to remind us of how badly and how often we miss the mark. Then he tempts us either to give up (disobedience) or to try harder (legalism). Can I get an amen?

So, if sin only increased when the Law came, why on earth did Paul emphatically declare that the Law is still holy "and the commandment is holy and righteous and good" (verse 12)? It's taking everything in me not to go all caps here, but the answer holds remarkable transforming power if you'll receive it: the Law is good and holy *when* it reveals my need of God and *when* that realization prompts me to celebrate the grace of Christ that has already and forever met the bar for me!

This is the party Paul threw in response to his own famous question, "Who will rescue me from this body of death?" (Romans 7:24, NIV). You may remember that Paul asked that question after mourning his inability to do what he wanted to do and his tendency to do what he didn't want to do! Scripture doesn't tell us anything about Paul's tone of voice when he dictated this letter, but I just have to believe he was shouting when he answered his own rhetorical question with this life-altering realization: "Thanks be to God—through Jesus Christ our Lord!" (verse 25).

Oh yes! Paul realized that the victory he desired could be secured through the gift of God—the indwelling presence of Jesus. Not once, but over and over, day in and day out in our pursuit of this holy God, we deal with this question: Will we trust Jesus and rest in His grace, or will we make and keep our own laws to try to feel better about ourselves?

Without a doubt, that question looms ever larger when we fail.

When we act as if our reinstatement into His good graces depends on how thoroughly we can repent, our foot has been taken in the trap of legalism. Consider the futile efforts we employ to make up for our failings—sort of like spiritual push-ups we assign ourselves. Lost your temper with the kids again? Looked at Facebook on your smartphone before you read the Bible? Or worse still, checked your Facebook messages *instead* of reading your Bible? These things alone could add up to twenty-five spiritual push-ups: ten minutes of reflecting on what a miserable Christian you are plus five minutes of extra-penitential prayer and an extra ten minutes of Bible reading tomorrow.

And that's just the self-punishment we mete out for what we consider small missteps. The greater our sin, the more isolated we feel from other believers, as well as from God, and the more penance we must perform. And heaven help us indeed if we don't *feel* forgiven. We're forced to go back to square one and repeat the steps. Most of us have become skilled at keeping our self-imposed penance a secret, but private or public, Legalism masquerading as Obedience stinks.

When we try to relate to God through the revelation of the Law (how holy God is and how holy we are not), we will work ourselves to death spiritually: "The mind of sinful man is death" (Romans 8:6a, NIV). By contrast, when we relate to Him through the Holy Spirit in us, understanding that we are accepted yesterday, today, and tomorrow, not because of anything we do or don't do but because of God's grace, we get life and peace: "but the mind controlled by the Spirit is life and peace" (Romans 8:6b, NIV).

Remember Becky, my friend who couldn't seem to let her husband lead until she closed her eyes and relaxed? It's vitally important that rather than try to orchestrate our spiritual progress, we surrender to the guiding hand of Jesus. Legalism wants us to set up our own standards instead of looking to The Standard. This is exactly what the Galatians were doing. Let it be known that if I could make this page begin flashing like one of those neon caution lights I mentioned earlier, I would! This next point is that crucial. However well-meaning our intentions, for us as believers to live in bondage to our own self-made laws is to be saved, sealed, and headed for heaven while starving for the sweet grace of Christ.

CLOSING THE DISTANCE

Are you familiar with the most fantabulous line of establishments known as Krispy Kreme Doughnuts? Their original glazed doughnut is a thing of beauty, made from a recipe that supposedly dates back to the 1930s. Had Shakespeare lived to see its day, we would undoubtedly have a classic sonnet along the lines of "Ode to the Krispy." Being as old Will has long since passed, allow me.

Long, long ago in a land of sugar and dough (okay, decades back in North Carolina, but I'm trying to be poetic), the bakery chain hit upon a stellar plan to lure customers into their stores. Each shop boasts a neon sign outside that flashes HOT NOW whenever the bakers pull a fresh batch of their sweet-as-nectar original glazed pastries from the oven. And, oh, do the hungry hordes take note! More than a few vehicular accidents have occurred at these intersections of busy street life and hot doughnuts.

What, you may well ask, has legalism to do with doughnuts? Sonnet aside, here's my point: Sometimes when I get my coffee and skip down to my favorite chair on the dock to enjoy some early morning prayer time with Jesus, I feel as if there's a great neon light outside the throne room blinking FELLOWSHIP AVAILABLE NOW. Oh, glory to God! On those days I waltz right on in. My heart seems to be in tune with His, and our communion easily picks up where we left off when I drifted to sleep the night before. On those days the fellowship is hot-doughnut sweet and fresh!

And then there are the other times.

Times when the heavens are like brass and my offerings fall right back down into my lap, times when my heart feels stubborn or resentful or unworthy and my mind wanders. (Perhaps you've picked up on the fact that my mind wanders more than the average bear.) On those days I begin to wonder what's wrong. *Hmmm...I didn't feel this distance yesterday.*

In an effort to muster up a good prayer mood, I am sometimes tempted to slip into old habits faster than you could say, "When will she learn?!" and I start analyzing myself again instead of focusing on Jesus. I listen to the Enemy's whisper. "Maybe your sins have separated you from God and He can't hear you." And my inward focus deepens. Sometimes the ancient snake takes the words Jesus once whispered at the gate of Gethsemane and twists them into a taunting accusation, "What? Can you not pray for one hour?" Try as I might to resist, my woebegone heart whispers, "Obviously not."

Did you know that Satan loves to take Scripture and beat us up with it? Well, now you do. Here's another fact: you can count on your Enemy to take God's words out of context and twist their meaning into an offensive dagger!

After all this time I still fall for his trap occasionally. I begin to examine myself and get lost in the study of me, me, me. I run through my mental archive, trying to figure out what I have or haven't done that could have created this distance from God. *Something is clearly wrong. Is it me? What did I do yesterday? What did I not do? What did I say? What did I not say?*

If I don't catch on to the Enemy's scheme, I can spend my entire prayer time trying to clean myself up enough, confess enough, repent enough, search my heart enough, and be focused enough to sense His presence enough...to pray. *Whew!* Trust me when I say it is as draining, repetitious, and defeating as it sounds.

Legalism's strength lies in luring us to spend our time and energy evaluating "me, myself, and I" rather than simply leaning into God's grace.

> **Introspection is healthy in small doses but debilitating if left unchecked.**

Without a doubt, Scripture teaches us to search out our own hearts. Paul challenged believers, "Test yourselves to see if you are in the faith; examine yourselves!" (2 Corinthians 13:5). And in Lamentations we read, "Let us examine and probe our ways, and let us return to the LORD" (3:40). So it is absolutely true that we're to examine ourselves and make sure we're living true to Christ's commands. But while introspection can be healthy in small doses, it's debilitating to our spiritual lives if left unchecked.

WHEN HEAVEN LEANS IN

I once saw an amusing headline: "Hypnotist Falls Under Own Spell." Of course I clicked on the link. This inquiring mind had to know more. To be sure, hypnotizing oneself sounded a little like something I might do if I was capable of putting anyone under my power, which I'm not—though I can think of a myriad of uses for that kind of skill.

Scanning the article, I learned the hypnotist was a newbie (surprise) who claimed to have accidentally put himself into a trance after practicing the ancient art for five straight hours while looking into a mirror. Southern or not, feel free to say this with me, "Bless his heart." Thankfully, the man's wife was able to contact his teacher/mentor for help in reaching her man. Afterward, Mr. Hypnotist promised that in the future he would practice autosuggestion under certain conditions: only if his Sweet Thang was present, and only if he had given her an agreed-upon word to release him in the event of another accident. (The article didn't say, but I'm thinking the odds are good the little woman may have suggested something along the lines of "Einstein" as his code word.)

That funny story is a spot-on illustration of the disastrous effects believers can suffer from too much introspection. Regular checkups are vital, but we aren't supposed to stare at ourselves indefinitely. Once we lay our hearts before God, it's every bit as crucial that we take our eyes off ourselves and determinedly focus them on Jesus. Ongoing self-consciousness leads us away from Christ instead of into His waiting arms. Consider these words from Jeremiah 17:7–10:

> Blessed is the man who trusts in the LORD
> And whose trust is the LORD.
> For he will be like a tree planted by the water,

That extends its roots by a stream
And will not fear when the heat comes;
But its leaves will be green,
And it will not be anxious in a year of drought
Nor cease to yield fruit.
The heart is more deceitful than all else
And is desperately sick;
Who can understand it?
I, the LORD, search the heart,
I test the mind,
Even to give to each man according to his ways,
According to the results of his deeds.

Getting me to trust in my evaluation of me, this is legalism's vicious trap. Scripture clearly teaches that we can't understand our own hearts or know everything that is in them. Our job is to go to God and trust Him to test our hearts and try them, to cleanse them and remake them after His own will.

> **Relying on Christ for salvation but using our evaluation of our own performance as the basis for fellowship will always frustrate His grace.**

Here's a favorite verse I memorized so I could repeat it to myself at the first sign that I'm getting sucked into the quicksand of introspection: "But if we walk in the light as He is in the light, we have fellowship with one another, and the blood of Jesus Christ His Son cleanses us from all sin" (1 John 1:7, NKJV).

Oh, do hold that one close and take comfort in its truth: the blood of Jesus *cleanses* us. Why is the tense of that verb so worthy of celebration?

Because it's an ongoing process. Our omnipotent, omnipresent, omniscient God is fully capable, faithful, and willing to tend to our hearts and bring up anything we need to address *as we walk in the light.*

I still have days when I try to pray and the words seem to bounce back, but I'm thankful that I now know what to do and what to avoid. When I feel distant from God, I refuse to let myself get stuck in the muck of me. As long as I'm in this body, the problem could be found in a hundred silly reasons, including what I did or did not eat the night before or how much rest I have or haven't gotten! I now know to call out to Him in naked desperation. I ask Him to search this needy heart and show me anything I need to tend to. Then I get busy feasting on all that is mine in Him. I proclaim aloud His matchless praises, recite my favorite verses, and take to Him my concerns and my thanksgivings, all the while trusting that He can hear my praise and my petitions even while simultaneously weeding my heart. When He brings something to mind that I need to confess, I simply confess, leave it there, and return to my worship with fresh cause to celebrate His faithfulness to forgive.

God is faithful to help us search our hearts if we ask. But once He has brought something to our minds and we've confessed it and received His forgiveness, we must learn to set our gaze squarely back on Jesus! When we begin to recount His worth, His glory, and His beauty and rejoice in all that is ours through Him, our cold hearts will thaw every time.

Those brass heavens we were discussing earlier—this is when they begin to part! He who sits on the throne, together with all the celestial inhabitants gathered around Him, leans in to hear the praises of Jesus, the Darling of heaven. When we take our eyes off ourselves and put them back on the Lamb, we land smack in the middle of heaven's ongoing celebration, as described by the apostle John:

Then I looked and heard the voice of many angels, numbering
thousands upon thousands, and ten thousand times ten thousand.
They encircled the throne and the living creatures and the elders. In a
loud voice they sang:

"Worthy is the Lamb, who was slain,
to receive power and wealth and wisdom and strength
and honor and glory and praise!"
    (Revelation 5:11–12, NIV)

Learning to take my eyes off myself and to trust solely in the finished
work of Christ has given me a taste of what it means to live before God—
and it has convinced me that the only way to stay free is to live as His slave.

THE SWEETEST SLAVERY

Remember when we settled that ownership issue in chapter 5? We established through Scripture that we have been bought with a price and if we
want to grow in our faith, if we want to walk and talk with Jesus, we don't
have the choice of whether or not to obey Him. Good. That slavery mentality is vital if we're going to stay untangled from our self-made laws.

Read with me these words from Ephesians, where we find Paul praying:

For this reason I kneel before the Father, from whom his whole family
in heaven and on earth derives its name. I pray that out of his glorious
riches he may strengthen you with power through his Spirit in your
inner being, so that Christ may dwell in your hearts through faith.
And I pray that you, being rooted and established in love, may have

power, together with all the saints, to grasp how wide and long and high and deep is the love of Christ, and to know this love that surpasses knowledge—that you may be filled to the measure of all the fullness of God. (3:14–19, NIV)

Did you notice Paul's heart for the saints to know the love of Christ that *surpasses* knowledge? I want you to be fully immersed in the love of Christ. God wants it for you more! The only way to sink down fully into Christ's love is to be His slave—to find our freedom and confidence in Jesus rather than our own efforts (see Ephesians 3:11–12). But I've learned that breaking the chains of self-consciousness is not a once-and-done formula. I need to regularly re-center my focus on the Cross of Christ; otherwise I'll find myself once again trying to approach God on the basis of my own success or failure. In doing so I will remain hungry for His presence, unable to close the gap and always disappointing myself. There is no middle ground to stand on here. When my gaze is held captive by the God Man, He frees me from the bully of me.

Let's contrast this practice of Christ-consciousness—keeping our eyes on who Jesus is and what He has done and continues to do for us—with the results of self-consciousness.

- Self-consciousness places a series of hurdles between us and God.
- Christ-consciousness defeats the devil's efforts to block our access to God's sweet company.
- Self-consciousness never finds the joy of worship.
- Christ-consciousness ushers us in.
- Self-consciousness keeps us seeking to muster up a sense of God's presence.
- Christ-consciousness lets us wake up and fall asleep in His presence.

- Self-consciousness tangles us up in introspection about me, mine, and ours.
- Christ-consciousness wraps us up in what God is doing and saying.

Are you beginning to see the picture? The strength of legalism can only be overcome through consciously and continuously centering our gaze on Christ. All our hope must be in Him, the object of our closest attention and highest affection. I quote Paul a lot because he taught me how to live free by identifying as a slave of Christ. It's how he so often introduced himself. In the following excerpt from his letter to the Roman church, Paul summed up the lifestyle that has Christ as its focus.

> Therefore I urge you, brethren, by the mercies of God, to present your bodies a living and holy sacrifice, acceptable to God, which is your spiritual service of worship. And do not be conformed to this world, but be transformed by the renewing of your mind, so that you may prove what the will of God is, that which is good and acceptable and perfect. (12:1–2)

In the original Greek language of the New Testament, the word translated here as *prove* means "to recognise as genuine after examination, to approve, deem worthy."[7] This is the blessing that awaits us when we yield to Christ and rely wholly on His finished work: we come to recognize for ourselves the good and acceptable and perfect will of God. This is the exuberant life of faith our hearts are designed to long for.

And yet, even as Paul describes the great blessing of this life in Christ, it's as if he can't help but remind his audience that it is theirs by grace and not as a result of anything they have done to earn it: "For through the grace given to me I say to everyone among you not to think more highly of himself than he ought to think; but to think so as to have sound judgment, as God has allotted to each a measure of faith" (verse 3).

BEGGARS OF MEN

If we don't practice Christ-consciousness, we won't know how to enter into God's presence for ourselves. Our enjoyment of Him will be forever limited to times of corporate fellowship, when we're in the company of other believers. Of course, worshiping God together with other Christians is a faith-enhancing experience that He expects us to practice regularly. Jesus Himself said, "Where two or more are gathered together in My name, I am there in the midst of them" (Matthew 18:20, NKJV). However—and I can't overstate the importance of this *however*—many of us are missing out on the intimacy we were meant to enjoy because we don't know how to avoid the trap of introspection and experience His company on our own time.

Do you know anyone who appears to love Jesus on Sunday but can't get it together Monday through Saturday? Right, I wouldn't necessarily want to answer that out loud either if I were you, especially since we've all been there, amen? But I want to suggest that instead of concluding that something is wrong with the faith of such believers (or with our own), we need to consider that their Sunday experience may be fully authentic. It's possible to truly enjoy worship while others are worshiping and to truly enjoy hearing the Word when others are breaking it into bite-size pieces for us, without ever learning to do these things for ourselves. But it's a tragic way for believers to live. If we stay there, we remain beggars of men, asking mere mortals for morsels from God.

Learning to approach God solely through confidence in Jesus Christ has been a lesson of epic proportions in my life. I find it impossible to make too much of it. This precious truth has impacted my faith in ways I am still discovering even today. It has positioned me to hear Him more clearly and know Him more dearly. I hope these words whet your thirst because I want this for you too.

> **Don't be a beggar of men, asking**
> **mere mortals for morsels from God.**

The joy of our great salvation largely turns on the understanding that Jesus is our all-access pass to God. "He came and preached peace to you who were far away and peace to those who were near. For through him we both have access to the Father by one Spirit" (Ephesians 2:17–18, NIV).

When we are convinced that the door stands open for us at all times simply because of who He is and what He's done, regardless of who we are or what we've done, we are well on our way to becoming addicted to His Presence. Expect to find yourself craving more and more of this divine relationship, because every moment we spend with Him leaves us seeking another. The dividends are incalculable.

Oh, friend, our brief lives on this earth are made up of what we spend our energy on. We can fill our days with rules and regrets, or we can kick Legalism in the shins and live with our hearts wide open in the beauty of unending grace. Don't struggle to know what is already yours! If we but run to God with Jesus the Big Ticket clutched in our sweaty palms, the door to God's presence will open to us every single time.

Dear God, help me to examine my heart and confess when I need to confess. But please don't let me get caught in the web of introspection that prevents me from learning to be with You! I know that I can't approach You on my own goodness or efforts, and I don't want to try! Please alert me when I start down that path. I know that Christ and Christ alone gives me access to You. Help me to fix my eyes on Jesus and celebrate His beauty along with all of heaven. Amen.

7

MAY WE HAVE PERMISSION TO SLAP 'EM SILLY IN JESUS'S NAME?

"Lord, other believers are treading on my last nerve. How am I supposed to love them?"

$\mathcal{S}$omewhere in the television cabinet crammed with video footage from Phillip's and Jessica's growing-up years lies the record of a troubled group performance from one of our daughter's long-ago dance recitals. The last time we ran across it, I vowed to pull the tape out and keep it where I could find it again. Unfortunately, I didn't follow through, so the clip is once again buried somewhere in the stacks of poorly labeled VHS videos I fully intend to organize one day. But that's okay. The film is forever frozen in my memory.

For this performance, Jessica and her tap-dancing buddies are dressed from head to toe in screaming canary yellow, each carrying a lacy parasol that is rarely opened or closed on cue. Several times during their big number, the little girls are supposed to turn right and skip-to-their-lous in a circle. Unfortunately, this part of the routine never goes well because one of the dancers keeps forgetting which way her lou is supposed to be skipping. Each time the line turns right, the poor child hangs a left. Jessica Ann spends the entire dance turning her confused cohort around by the shoulders and nudging her in the right direction, even as she tries valiantly to keep pace with the music and the other girls' steps. Aggravated by her fellow dancer, embarrassed in front of the audience, yet eager to perform her much-anticipated number, Jessica perseveres, but her conflicting emotions can be read all over her five-year-old face.

Dare we admit that we can relate? Sometimes it seems that living for God would be a whole lot easier if the people around us would just act right. To turn the other cheek requires great determination when those who spurn God ridicule us for seeking Him. Whether the derision comes from a family member or a coworker, being mocked or stereotyped for our faith can leave us frustrated at best and shaken at worse. But let's be honest: we often find ourselves much more agitated about the person in the next pew who worships the same God! Here, I'll go first and take the heat off you.

I've been guilty of thinking less than Jesus-like thoughts about people who are immediately skeptical of anything the church does that isn't done exactly as it was in the past. On the other hand, I get just as irritated by people who can't appreciate the spiritual wisdom of yesterday's saints and think we have to throw out old revelations to embrace what God is saying today. I quickly grow exasperated with believers who criticize the way others worship or frown on the Bible translation others embrace. And how's this for a real-life confession: I don't appreciate the people who never volunteer to help but always know how the conference, retreat, or baby shower should be run. Can you relate?

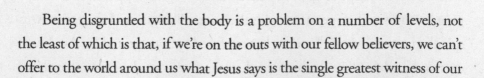

Loving one another is the single greatest witness of our faith to the unbelieving world around us.

Being disgruntled with the body is a problem on a number of levels, not the least of which is that, if we're on the outs with our fellow believers, we can't offer to the world around us what Jesus says is the single greatest witness of our faith. "A new commandment I give to you, that you love one another, even as I have loved you, that you also love one another. By this all men will know that you are My disciples, if you have love for one another" (John 13:34–35).

Perhaps if we were hermits, we could live out that fine commandment without gnawing holes in our tongues. But here in the real world, someone somewhere is going to stomp all over our good intentions, whether in private or under the embarrassing glare of public lights. That said, Scripture is clear: if our goal is to enjoy the passionate presence of God, we'd best figure out this "love one another" thing.

> If someone says, "I love God," and hates his brother, he is a liar; for the one who does not love his brother whom he has seen, cannot love God whom he has not seen. And this commandment we have from Him, that the one who loves God should love his brother also." (1 John 4:20–21)

In other words, we can't love God without loving each other. If it helps, I promise you'll have endless opportunities to practice!

PETER SIDES WITH MAMA

My sisters and I spent a lot of time in trouble when we were little. We also spent a lot of time at church. Hence, we spent a lot of time in trouble at church. The topic of how we love our fellow believers brings to mind one of the many times we girls broke a commandment. It wasn't one of God's Big Ten, but it was listed in Mama's book, and she was nearly as swift as the Almighty Himself at meting out punishment. It all began one Sunday evening as the deacons started passing out communion.

Cyndie, Rhonda, and I knew the ropes here. Take a piece of bread, wait for the prayer, watch the pastor and the deacons, and eat when they eat. Next, take a tiny thimble of grape juice, wait for the prayer, watch the preacher and the deacons, and swig when they swigged.

This particular day a visitor who apparently lacked our wealth of church experience was seated across the aisle from us. As soon as she got her juice, the visitor began to sip it daintily with her pinky finger extended, looking like the Queen Mum at high tea. We girls were having trouble maintaining our composure in light of this breach of protocol. Then she looked our way and lifted her glass in a toasting manner, as if to say, "It's quite good. Have some." The short version: we lost it, and Mama made us pay dearly for laughing at our well-meaning but uninformed visitor during the observance of Holy Communion!

I can't help thinking the apostle Peter would have had Mama's back on that one, given the sort of training regimen he laid out for growing in Christian virtues. Do take note of where he parked godliness: "Make every effort to supplement your faith with goodness, goodness with knowledge, knowledge with self-control, self-control with endurance, endurance with godliness, godliness with brotherly affection, and brotherly affection with love" (2 Peter 1:5–7, HCSB).

Isn't that interesting? The list of personal attributes we're encouraged to add to our faith is capped off with brotherly affection and love. And get this: the prompt comes while we're working on our godliness. I view this as a reminder that, throughout the Scriptures, the importance of love for our fellow believers is woven so tightly with personal faith as to be inseparable! Over and over we see echoes of Jesus's call to the love that should mark us as believers, reminders that love is the supreme virtue for those who follow Him:

Therefore I, the prisoner of the Lord, implore you to walk in a manner worthy of the calling with which you have been called, with all

146

humility and gentleness, with patience, showing tolerance for one
another in love. (Ephesians 4:1–2)

Only conduct yourselves in a manner worthy of the gospel of Christ,
so that whether I come and see you or remain absent, I will hear of
you that you are standing firm in one spirit, with one mind striving
together for the faith of the gospel. (Philippians 1:27)

Above all, keep fervent in your love one for another. (1 Peter 4:8)

Let all that you do be done in love. (1 Corinthians 16:14)

If I speak with the tongues of men and of angels, but do not have love, I
have become a noisy gong or a clanging cymbal. (1 Corinthians 13:1)

And, of course, when asked to speak to the greatest of all commandments, Jesus fused our love for God and our love for one another into one
shining golden standard: "'Love the Lord your God with all your heart and
with all your soul and with all your mind.' This is the first and greatest commandment. And the second is like it: 'Love your neighbor as yourself'"
(Matthew 22:37–39, NIV).

It doesn't take a Bible scholar to see that God intends for us to walk in
love, but I suspect you already knew that. Perhaps we should fast-forward to
the application.

In Psalm 16 King David offered another great lesson for those of us already sold on the need-to for brotherly love but short on the how-to:

Oh my soul, you have said to the LORD,
"You are my Lord,

My goodness is nothing apart from You."

As for the saints who are on the earth,

"They are the excellent ones, in whom is all my delight."

(verses 2–3, NKJV)

Let's stop right there. David just said that he *delighted* in the saints. According to other translations, the good king called the godly people he knew *majestic, splendid,* and *noble.* Now, it would be a flat-out waste of time for anyone to try to convince me that the saints doing life with David didn't get on the good king's last nerve every now and then. These people put their sandals on the same way we do. So, if their sublime perfection wasn't fueling David's appreciation, what was? The answer is found in verse 2: "You are my Lord, my goodness is nothing apart from You." There it is! David's appreciation for his fellow saints was tied directly to his humble understanding of God's love for him.

David was able to enjoy his fellow saints despite their shortcomings because he realized that his own goodness was nothing apart from God. This, my friend, is a picture of how you and I will learn to walk in love. The more we celebrate the unmerited grace we've been given, the more easily we'll be able to extend it to others.

I once read a story about Saint Francis of Assisi that etched into my heart forever a visual expression of grace-propelled love. While walking alone on a narrow stretch of road, Saint Francis saw a leper approaching. The friar was terrified of contracting leprosy, and yet here he was in close proximity to a man whose entire flesh was white with the contagious and disfiguring disease. Wanting to turn away but deeply ashamed of himself for even thinking that way, Saint Francis instead ran toward the man to embrace him and to kiss the cheek of the startled leper. After their embrace, and as the men continued on their separate ways, Saint Francis turned for one last look at the poor leper. Behind him stretched an empty road. The leper was nowhere in sight. For the rest of his life, Saint Francis believed it was Christ Himself who met him in the road.

> The more we celebrate grace, the more easily we'll be able to extend it to others.

In the discourse on brotherly love found in 1 John, we are told that "God is love" and we can "love, because He first loved us" (1 John 4:16, 19). Crazy, often confounding, new and improved love—this is the everyday life God expects of us because Christ has made it possible.

LOVE, NEW AND IMPROVED

In essence, that's the really good, simply divine reason why loving our fellow believers isn't merely a nice idea or passing suggestion. We're fully equipped to keep just such a commandment! Remember the words of Jesus in the book of John that we looked at earlier? "A new commandment I give to you, that you love one another, even as I have loved you, that you also love one another. By this all men will know that you are My disciples, if you have love for one another" (13:34–35). Let's dig a little deeper into those red-letter words.

It's worth noting that Jesus gave this new commandment during His last evening with the twelve disciples. Judas and Jesus had just finished what seemed a most cryptic exchange to those listening, and then Judas abruptly left the upper room. There in the company of only His closest and most loyal friends, Jesus announced that the time had come for Him to be glorified and for Him to glorify the Father. He told the men that where He was going they couldn't follow, and the very next words that came out of His mouth revealed this "new" commandment: they were to love one another as He had loved them.

It is essential to our understanding of this verse to keep in mind that Jesus's listeners were Jews first. These guys would have known the Old Testament command to "love your neighbor as yourself" inside and out. They'd been thoroughly steeped in the wording of the Law as well as in the how and why of the command: "You shall not take vengeance, nor bear any grudge against the sons of your people, but you shall love your neighbor as yourself; I am the LORD" (Leviticus 19:18).

So why did Jesus call this a "new" commandment, especially after having already identified the greatest commandments—to love God and love one another? I hope you're reading this somewhere that is conducive to a little shouting because you may feel the need to get boisterous. I know I do! The *Holman Illustrated Bible Dictionary* defines *new* as something "different from one of the same which existed before; made fresh."[8] This commandment to love one another isn't something new as in "something previously unheard of"; it is new as in "improved"! In other words, the great new advantage would be Jesus living in His followers in the form of the Holy Spirit, making it possible to keep the second greatest of all the commandments. Christ in us empowers us to love as God loves!

Wonderful! So, that's just going to happen automatically, right? Absolutely—in our dreams. Once we wake up we'll still run into button pushers who seem gifted in knowing when, where, and how hard to press to prompt a reaction.

Can we really love and keep loving? Yes, we can. We can love from the bottomless well of Christ if we change our perspective and see every one of these needy moments as a glorious opportunity to run back to the throne! *Fill me up again, Lord! You told me to love and then You made it so I could! Help me live it out.*

It almost seems a shame to follow this celebration of the new and improved Love with our next story, but it paints too good an illustration of the big fail that results when we try to love out of our own efforts.

THERE'S A NAME FOR OUR WEAKNESS

"Shhh… It's okay. Just close your eyes and rest." It's been years since I whispered those comforting words into my infant granddaughter's ears as I stroked her baby-fine hair and tried in vain to choke back the tears that stung my eyes. That little one is five years old now, but I well remember her bottom lip quivering as she hiccuped and wailed her woe-is-me cries. Emerson's distress wrung my heart out like a dishrag then, and it can still do so today. But that particular morning, my heart was gripped by the startling familiarity of the moment. I had recently whispered those very same words to another loved one, only in a vastly different setting.

"Shhh… It's okay. Just close your eyes and rest." The night before I'd been stroking thin gray hair and trying to comfort my aged mother-in-law. At age eighty-one, Lucy's body was giving up after a lengthy battle with Alzheimer's that had long since stolen her mind. Where we'd once been able to laugh together at the little things Mawmaw said in her confusion, the sadness of watching her move into the ever-darkening tunnel that marks that dreaded disease now threatened to eclipse all traces of joy.

I'll never forget the irony of comforting Mawmaw one moment and Emerson the next, trying to soothe both with the same words and sounds. "Shhh… It's okay. Just close your eyes and rest." There was something so weighty there, and something incredibly sweet. Even as I comforted Emerson and wondered what lay ahead in her journey, that morning I suddenly realized that I was *blessed by God* to be able to comfort Mawmaw at the end of hers. Tending Lucy at the end of her life was a gift, an opportunity to give love with zero expectation of return. The realization brought me to my knees.

This is where we must hit Pause. In the event that you're picturing me as some Louisiana version of Mother Teresa, eagerly tending to my mother-in-law day and night, I want to be perfectly clear about what brought me to my knees. Well, I don't actually want to come clean, but it's necessary. You see, some days I had plenty of love and patience for the demands of Mawmaw Lucy's last years, along with all the other responsibilities life was throwing at me. However, as painful as it is to put this in black and white, other times I felt overburdened, stressed out, and put upon faster than you could say, "Aren't you ashamed of yourself?" On those days, I was capable of coming and going from Lucy's bedside in rote service with a cold and unaffected heart. Ugh. Admitting that hurts all over again. But remembering that I can be holey more often than I'm holy keeps me running to Jesus, who freely gives grace that I might freely pass it on.

Did I want to have an abundance of grace on hand during those twilight years with Lucy? Of course I did. Just as surely as I want to live with plentiful grace for those who are doing life with me today. Seeing as you're hanging in here, I believe you want to have grace on hand for your friends and family too. Excellent! That should make the hard truth a little easier to take.

> ## Knowing I can be holey more often than I'm holy keeps me running to Jesus.

There's really no gentle way to address it, so we'll just lay this thing out in the open. You and I have an Achilles heel that hinders us as we seek to follow God, and it makes it difficult for us to let His love flow freely in and through us.

The dictionary defines an Achilles heel as a weakness that seems to be small when it is actually crucial.[9] It's a spot-on analogy of the prevailing problem that trips up many an unsuspecting saint. Thankfully, it doesn't have to be a permanent weakness. Let's name the thing so we can address it: the believer's Achilles heel is our tendency to store up offenses when we should be stockpiling grace.

Consider my mother-in-law. On any given day, if I was actively laying my heart before Jesus to be cleansed, repaired, and refueled, I had grace for whatever was required—and that included caring for Mawmaw. If I let Him tend my heart, I had love available and handy to pass along. However, if I came to the situation nursing a wound of my own, trying to love on my mother-in-law was like attempting to run a marathon with a torn Achilles tendon. What I needed just wasn't there!

> Every word or act we can't forgive is a
> word or act we are bound to relive.

So why is it that we continue to delude ourselves into thinking we can store an offense in one corner of our lives without it affecting another? Not one of us would purposely hoard rotten food in her pantry. We know one rancid potato quickly taints the whole bag. We know the pantry will soon begin to smell, and if the potato is left long enough, flies will hatch, swarm, and invade the rest of our provisions. And yet we manage to convince ourselves that the wounds of offense we're nursing are relatively small and inconsequential. We pretend the bitterness isn't tainting our relationships when it actually is suffocating our spirits. Every word or act we can't forgive is a word or act we are bound to relive, and with each remembrance the bitterness spreads deeper into our souls.

We simply can't partition our hearts into isolated pockets, with unresolved people issues in one corner and passionate love for God in another—

and expect one not to affect the other. "A little yeast works through the whole batch of dough" (Galatians 5:9, NIV).

The only prescription for walking in love with people is to live wholly open to Love Himself so that He might continually tend our hearts and keep us from nursing an Achilles heel that might trip us up or sideline us entirely.

The apostle Paul underscored this great truth in Galatians 5. He summed up the whole Law as being fulfilled in one commandment, to love our neighbor as we love ourselves, and then in the same breath he cautioned believers, "If you keep on biting and devouring each other, watch out or you will be destroyed by each other" (verse 15, NIV). Who us, Paul? Excuse me for laughing, but the short answer is "Yes, indeed." The letter was addressed to the churches of Galatia, but our names might as well be right there in black and white.

"She Makes Me Want to Shout!"

If you'll allow me to apply a little imagination to the scene, I can bring that ancient assembly of new believers into focus. I see one of the new converts rolling her eyes while Paul's letter is read aloud. She's deep in thought about that bur-under-the-donkey-blanket woman sitting across the room, the one who makes her want to shout, and not in a hallelujah way. I can hear someone else coughing loudly in the direction of another fellow who really needs to hear this particular message of Paul's in the worst way. That's all conjecture on my part, of course, but what happened next is on the record. After warning his listeners about the dangers of sniping at one another, the apostle wasted no time launching into the antidote: Walk in the Spirit, y'all, and you won't fulfill the desire of the flesh (see verse 16).

You're right. He didn't say *y'all*. The scripture is just so familiar I tend to hear it in my own dialect. Interestingly enough, however, I had never noticed this *desire of the flesh* warning parked right there with the infighting until I studied brotherly kindness. I think I had always associated the caution with other fleshly desires, such as coveting material things or pursuing ill-advised relationships. But Paul's point wasn't so narrow and neatly packaged. He wanted us to know that Christ is living in us to redeem our sinful nature. He equips us to act not out of our own hearts but out of God's love—if we have yielded to His Spirit.

Where we fail is trying to force through the right response in our own power. The late comedian Henny Youngman used to tell a joke about a man who went to his doctor and said, "Doc, it hurts when I poke right here. What should I do?" To which the doctor replied, "Don't poke right there!" It's an oldie but goodie that reminds me of the biblical truth found in 2 Corinthians 10:5: "We are destroying speculations and every lofty thing raised up against the knowledge of God, and we are taking every thought captive to the obedience of Christ."

Over and over we poke the same thoughts and act surprised when the pain makes us flinch.

> Our thought lives can trap us in a death spiral
> that drains the love of God right out of us.

Taking our thoughts captive has got to be one of the most powerful, freeing behaviors a believer can learn. My problem is that I've been known to take a thought captive all right—captive as in, "You're not getting away from me now, you irritating, frustrating, and defeating thought. I'm not through thinking on you yet!" Perhaps you can relate?

I can analyze a thought to death while simultaneously trying to free myself from its death grip. And that deadly reference was most intentional. Our thought lives can trap us in a death spiral that drains the love of God right out of us. Our only hope of escaping the vortex is to keep reading beyond the first half of that well-known verse to the power that lies in the second half: "And we are taking every thought captive *to the obedience of Christ.*"

The obedience of Christ, that's the muscle we need to succeed. Thankfully, I'm learning that the only way to escape a thought is to bring it under the dominion of Christ. All my efforts are wasted until I lay it before Jesus. That's where it gets defeated. When I say, "Lord, I want to give up this hurt, this pattern of thinking, but I'm powerless to do it on my own. Please give me strength to let it be," that's when the glorious power of Christ becomes available to break the pattern.

"Do You Want to Get Well?"

I was born with an underdeveloped rib cage. I recall Mama saying that a grownup's fist could fit easily in the small valley in the middle of my chest. Throughout my childhood, the doctors would reexamine the little hollow over my heart and remind my parents that just the right blow to that area of my chest could have serious repercussions.

My concerned mama sternly laid the law down to my older sisters. Cyndie and Rhonda were to be ever so careful to see that I didn't get hit in the chest. During the course of our childhood squabbles, they complied by beating me up in less obvious places, until I realized what a stroke of good fortune my little abnormality presented. I discovered that by threatening to tell Mama that one of them had hit me in the chest, regardless of whether or not she actually had, I could either get my way or see to it that my sisters got a spanking, thereby successfully turning my challenge into my sisters' nightmare. As embarrassing as it is to admit, it wasn't the only time I used my vulnerability to advantage.

My right arm took some abuse when I was growing up, all of it self-inflicted and accidental. For a time I was the poster child for the uncoordinated. I fractured that arm skating, and I cracked it doing gymnastics, but the first time I broke it, I was a preschooler running down the driveway when I tripped over my spaghetti legs and went rolling like a tumbleweed.

Back then they made casts out of sure-enough plaster, none of this wimpy lightweight stuff. We're talking heavy-duty help for injured skeletons. I'm pretty sure that first big white cast outweighed me. I quickly grew tired of lugging it around. It was uncomfortable and it itched. However, I discovered it could serve me well in one particular way.

Whenever my older sisters started to aggravate me, which seldom happened unless they were awake, I could hit them over the head with it—whack! Of course, I got in trouble for these acts of violence. Mama said I was my own worst enemy and my arm would never heal if I used it like a weapon. She was right as usual, but even so, when the cast came off, I couldn't help being just a little sad to see it go.

Let's be honest: as grownups we use our weaknesses and wounds to hurt others too, don't we? If we've suffered betrayal, we might wield our emotions as weapons to prompt others to give us a wider berth than usual. When life leaves us a bit battered, we may be tempted to adopt the attitude that a little rudeness to others is justified after all we've been through. And when people gather round to show us kindness and love during a difficult season, we sometimes can grow used to being the center of all the attention and the recipient of all that casserole giving.

So let me get personal here for a moment and invite you to think long and hard about something. Do you want to get well?

Jesus asked that very question of a man in the fifth chapter of John's gospel. The setting was a pool called Bethesda, which was said to be stirred by angels at certain seasons. Whoever stepped into the moving waters first would be healed. One particular man had lain by the pool for many years, never able to reach the pool in time because he didn't have anyone to help him in. It was this broken, lonely man whom Jesus addressed with our question, "Do you want to get well?" (John 5:6, NIV).

If it weren't Jesus asking the question, we might think it a heartless inquiry. But Love Himself stood waiting for the man's answer. Why had He even asked? Well, for the man at Bethesda, healing might have brought consequences that the fellow hadn't fully considered. Perhaps Jesus was giving him a heads-up: You won't be able to beg for a living anymore. You won't have an excuse for the way you act right now. Are you sure you're ready for that?

I think Love Himself often asks us the same question. Do you want to get well, or are you too accustomed to using your pain to beat up those closest to you to trade it in?

We grow so comfortable with our anger over an unkind comment or action that it seems impossible to let it go. We adopt heartache as part of our identity, daring others to even attempt encouragement. Emotional blackmail imprisons everyone involved. We become so comfortable with our wounds and their wrappings that we cheat ourselves of the healing God offers. You know, my arm was pale and scrawny when that cast was finally removed, and it took some time to regain any strength, but it really did feel good to be whole and unencumbered again. So, too, our spirits can live whole and free if we'll let the Great Physician take away the pain we're toting.

Are you harboring a hurt that is supersensitive to the touch? Remember our doctor joke and resist the urge to poke it. Don't pet it, harbor it, or analyze it. Run to the Cross with it and feel its sting fade away.

THE HIP BONE'S CONNECTED TO THE THIGH BONE

When we learn to continually resort to Jesus and draw on His empowering grace to love and forgive one another, we experience another of those win-wins. Our obedience heals us while it simultaneously opens us up to enjoy a host of divine blessings as we walk in love with our brothers and sisters.

You're likely familiar with the Scripture's teaching that we are members of one body:

> Now the body is not made up of one part but of many.... And if the ear should say, "Because I am not an eye, I do not belong to the body," it would not for that reason cease to be part of the body. If the whole body were an eye, where would the sense of hearing be? If the whole body were an ear, where would the sense of smell be? (1 Corinthians 12:14, 16–17, NIV)

I find it sad that this wonderful passage is quoted most often to soothe our little Christian egos. We use Paul's discourse on the body to encourage ourselves that the toe is as important as the hand and so on. This is the church's go-to passage to keep down jealousy and make everyone feel good about his or her place in the body.

While it's certainly true that none of us is more important than the other, might I suggest, as gently as possible, that by stopping there, we miss Paul's message on the value of brotherly love and unity? As that passage progresses, we read, "The eye cannot say to the hand, 'I don't need you!' And the head cannot say to the feet, 'I don't need you!'" (verse 21).

We've often seen this passage as a way to make the individual members feel better about themselves, but the close of the passage suggests the true purpose: "But God has combined the members of the body and has given greater honor to the parts that lacked it, *so that there should be no division in the body, but that its parts should have equal concern for each other*" (verses 24–25, emphasis added).

Paul went on to talk about the body suffering together and rejoicing together and the different gifts of the Spirit that profit the church as a whole. And then, after encouraging his readers to desire the greater gifts, he launched into what is commonly known as The Love Chapter, which celebrates the greatest gift of all: "And now I will show you the most excellent way. If I speak in the tongues of men and of angels, but have not love, I am only a resounding gong or a clanging cymbal" (12:31–13:1, NIV).

To walk in love with the body of Christ is indeed "the most excellent way." It leads us to a richer, more abundant life, as does every instruction God asks us to obey. In short, obedience to God makes life worth living!

We opened this chapter talking about King David and his love for his brethren. With the exception of Jesus, I'm not sure any mortal soul has ever celebrated the joy of obeying God as fully as David did. This is not a man who was satisfied to grit his teeth and obey God with a sour expression on his face. Far from taking a stiff-upper-lip approach to following God's Word, David thrilled to the opportunity of getting in on what God expected from man. In Psalm 19 he espoused the beauty of his discovery:

> The law of the LORD is perfect, restoring the soul;
> The testimony of the LORD is sure, making wise the
>   simple.
> The precepts of the LORD are right, rejoicing the heart;
> The commandment of the LORD is pure, enlightening
>   the eyes.
> The fear of the LORD is clean, enduring forever;
> The judgments of the LORD are true, they are righteous
>   altogether.
> They are more desirable than gold, yes, than much fine
>   gold;

Sweeter also than honey and the drippings of the honey-
comb. (verses 7–10)

Tell me, does that sound like someone who follows rules and regulations because it is expected—or someone who has learned that God's way is the only way to roll? We need to take a cue from the one God called a man after His own heart and etch this truth in our souls: to experience the full, overflowing life of the indwelling Spirit of Christ, we need to understand that whatever He asks of us—and in this case we're talking about loving our spiritual sisters and brothers—is a get-to and not a have-to!

We noted earlier that God will never make a single request of us that is not for us. Jesus's direction to love one another is no exception. When we walk in love, we not only contribute to the overall health of the body of Christ and stimulate its growth but also find our individual faith strengthened. Consider the challenge offered by the writer of Hebrews:

Let us hold fast the confession of our hope without wavering, for He
who promised is faithful; and let us consider how to stimulate one
another to love and good deeds, not forsaking our own assembling
together, as is the habit of some, but encouraging one another; and
all the more as you see the day drawing near. (10:23–25)

Do you see it? We're called to not merely tolerate each other but actually inspire one another to greater expressions of love. We have a joyful responsibility to our brothers and sisters.

But encourage one another daily, as long as it is called Today, so
that none of you may be hardened by sin's deceitfulness. (Hebrews
3:13, NIV)

I need you. You need me. Our mutual love for each other stimulates our growth in Christ and protects us from the deceptive tactics of the Enemy. Note the end of this next passage.

> But speaking the truth in love, we are to grow up in all aspects into
> Him who is the head, even Christ, from whom the whole body, being
> fitted and held together by what every joint supplies, according to the
> proper working of each individual part, causes the growth of the body
> for the building up of itself in love. (Ephesians 4:15–16)

And so our obedience to this great commandment to love one another, which we first saw as our dutiful witness to the world, then as the substance of our own healing, turns out to be yet another of God's incredible provisions for us. We are one another's assets. God wants to use the love of other members of His body to build us up and help us in our passionate pursuit of Him.

Let's Go Hunting!

I type these words to you on a beautiful fall day. Right now my men are knee-deep in the farming season, but don't think for a minute that they haven't already begun to dream about hunting season.

Last year my husband, Phil, and my son, Phillip, managed to see several extremely big bucks—we're talking trophy-size specimens, potential record breakers. Unfortunately, they were all on the Internet. That may seem a lame attempt at humor (and it probably is), but if you happen to live with a committed hunter, you understand all too well the obsession that takes hold. My own sweet hunters are lightning fast with the deer-related e-mail forwards. Once I clicked on an e-mail from my son-in-law, who lives in Houston.

Patrick had attached to his note a photo of a large trophy buck that a friend of a friend of a friend had just taken down in Louisiana. As it happens, that very photo was already printed out and resting on my snack bar. Like so many of his deer friends, that buck was making the Internet rounds.

I've noticed that about hunters. Even when they aren't having any success of their own, they get excited to hear from those who are. A friend's success makes them want to go hunting that much more. In much the same way, when you let me in on your hunt for All Things Jesus, whether it's the hope you've gained from a newly discovered treasure in His Word or a victory His grace has wrought in you, your experiences urge me to keep seeking.

This circle of encouragement can be found in Paul's letter to the Roman church. "For I long to see you so that I may impart some spiritual gift to you, that you may be established; that is, that I may be encouraged together with you while among you, each of us by the other's faith, both yours and mine" (Romans 1:11–12).

Indeed, the evidence of God in your life breeds excitement in mine. Or to put it in terms my camo-wearing men would relate to, your success makes me want to go hunting!

> **Your experiences with God urge me to keep seeking Him.**

We can and we should begin to see each other as assets in our thirst for God. I want to learn how to articulate for you what I'm hearing from God, and I want you to do the same for me. I believe every single one of us is born with the potential to display an aspect of the Father's personality that is uniquely ours to share. We are each other's opportunity to trace His hands and feet in this world so that together we may draw closer to Him and see more of His glory.

Dear God, I want to learn to not simply endure my fellow believers but to treasure them as the assets they are in my walk with You. Teach me to tank up on grace instead of storing offenses. Help me remember to run to You for the power to take those painful thoughts captive. According to Your Word, my fellow believers can help strengthen my faith if I learn to appreciate them—and I have the privilege of helping to strengthen theirs in return. Help me love them the way You love me. Amen.

8

TILL WE SEE HIM FACE TO FACE

few years ago my small hometown swelled to overflow capacity as forty years of Briarfield Academy alumni returned for one ginormous reunion. Some folks had changed a lot, physically speaking, which gave us all ample opportunity to play Name That Alumnus. Identifying labels had been provided, mind you, but way too many clowns insisted on covering their name tags and asking, "Who am I?" Several times I joked in response, "Well, if you'll move your hand and step back a pace so my middle-aged eyes can focus, I may be able to help you!"

On the other hand, those who stayed in touch had no trouble recognizing one another in the crowd. That's the lesson of a relationship built through ongoing companionship compared to one with a shared history and nothing more than yesterday's memories. It's also a revealing metaphor for our faith.

If all we have with the Lord is a history based on the memory of when we first believed, we may as well be friendly strangers. We won't recognize His touch or hear His voice. This doesn't have to be, and it's not meant to be.

I've heard people tell brand-new believers that they might not always feel so "high" on Christ (for lack of a better word) as the day when they first believed. These Jesus babies are urged to be careful to remember "that moment" when they first believed so that if they should ever begin to doubt their new faith, they can return to it for comfort and peace of mind. I'm convinced that the people who say such things mean well, but let's stop and think for a minute just how it must grieve our almighty, omnipotent God. We are telling new believers to expect the fade!

Father, forgive us. May such poor advice never pass our lips again! As we near the close of our time together in the pages of this book, I want to be absolutely sure you understand that I am still dealing with the same ups and downs that you face. I don't wake up, walk out, and turn in my days without my share of problems. I find my attitude needing frequent adjustment and my heart needing realignment, and I don't expect that to change on this side of glory.

I'd be foolish to suggest that we can't grow stale or discouraged, not when the Word tells us to "fan into flame the gift of God" (2 Timothy 1:6, NIV) and to "encourage one another day after day" (Hebrews 3:13). But it is also undeniably true that we can search the Scriptures till Jesus returns, and we'll never find a single verse even remotely suggesting that we're destined to live with some sort of fading glory from the hour we first believed!

Oh, that we would challenge every new believer with this scriptural truth: the moment we allow ourselves to be embraced by Christ is only the beginning of His work in us, the first taste of a life far and above what the world calls living.

Let's tell them the One who saves us wants to reveal Himself to us more fully day by day until we meet Him face to face. (Or face to ground, as the case will surely be when we get our first unveiled view of God in His glory! I suspect that none of us have begun to understand the great kindness of Christ Jesus shown to us by this invitation to share His glory forever.)

Something momentous has happened since I first began writing these words about the great travesty of low expectations. The timing prompts me to contemplate yet again the beautiful, mysterious ways of our God, and I'm just longing to bring you in on it.

While in the throes of determining never to take part in passing along such pessimistic counsel, God gave me the incredible gift of being able to pray with a precious young woman to embrace the forgiveness and grace that is hers through Christ Jesus. At the very moment of her new birth, I was able to share with her the message I'd been thinking on and writing about. "This," I told my new sister in Christ, "this is only day one. Day one, I tell you! Don't listen to anyone who says this will likely be the pinnacle of your relationship to Jesus. You do not have to lose this joy. You have a choice in the matter! Run hard after Jesus today, tomorrow, and the day after that, and you can discover the delights of an increasingly close relationship with Him."

When He was getting ready to leave this earth, Jesus told His followers, "I have much more to say to you, more than you can now bear. But when he, the Spirit of truth, comes, he will guide you into all truth. He will not speak on his own; he will speak only what he hears, and he will tell you what is yet to come" (John 16:12–13, NIV).

The Holy Spirit living in us, teaching us things we don't know, mysteries downloaded straight from heaven concerning what's going on right now and what's headed our way. Does that sound to you like the fading glow of a ho-hum Christian life?

A DIVINE PRODUCTION

Finite thinkers that we are, we need to ask God to help us understand that our birth in Christ is just that, a divine starting place without a finish line. You might be thinking, *Wait, Shellie, didn't the great apostle Paul write about finishing his race?* He most certainly did. One day you and I will finish our earthly course too, but crossing the finish line that delivers us into the presence of God will only be our first step into an eternity with Him! Can we even begin to understand that we'll need all of eternity to worship this Being, the One heaven's angels have praised from before the foundation of our world without once getting their fill of the holy celebration?

To illustrate my point, I want us to take in a scene from heaven together. It's found in the fourth chapter of the book of Revelation. We'll be jumping feet first into John the apostle's description of the sights he saw and the sounds he heard when he was transported from the isle of Patmos to a front-row seat in glory. It might help if we could sit back and imagine ourselves in padded theater chairs, sharing a tub of hot buttered popcorn as we watch the scene come to life on a big screen.

Are you ready? Okay, hold on tight, and I'll hit the Play button. The opening credits might read...

A Divine Production

From the Holy Spirit–Inspired Pen of John the Apostle

As the scene opens we're treated to a bird's-eye view of another world. Images glisten on the screen like a 3-D film on steroids. As our eyes drink in colors sharper than any we've ever seen, the camera settles on a door. It stands open, and we find ourselves leaning toward it as the narrator begins to speak.

> After these things I looked, and behold, a door standing open in heaven, and the first voice which I had heard, like the sound of a trumpet speaking with me, said, "Come up here, and I will show you what must take place after these things."
>
> Immediately I was in the Spirit; and behold, a throne was standing in heaven, and One sitting on the throne. (Revelation 4:1–2)

The musical soundtrack builds as the camera takes us through the door, and we're transfixed with wonder at the first sight of the main character, The Ancient of Days.

> And He who was sitting was like a jasper stone and a sardius in appearance; and there was a rainbow around the throne, like an emerald in appearance. Around the throne were twenty-four thrones; and upon the thrones I saw twenty-four elders sitting, clothed in white garments, and golden crowns on their heads. (verses 3–4)

We remind ourselves to breathe. There's no way we'll ever be able to describe what we're experiencing. Our friends will have to see this for themselves! A loud crash of lightning strikes the screen as thunder rocks us in our seats.

> Out from the throne come flashes of lightning and sounds and peals of thunder. And there were seven lamps of fire burning before the throne, which are the seven Spirits of God; and before the throne there was something like a sea of glass, like crystal; and in the center and around the throne, four living creatures full of eyes in front and behind. The first creature was like a lion, and the second creature like a calf, and the third creature had a face like that of a man, and the fourth creature was like a flying eagle. And the four living creatures, each one of them having six wings, are full of eyes around and within; and day and night they do not cease to say,
>
> "HOLY, HOLY, HOLY IS THE LORD GOD, THE ALMIGHTY,
>
> WHO WAS AND WHO IS AND WHO IS TO COME."
>
> (verses 5–8)

Our popcorn has long since been forgotten, along with everyone else around us. The only One who matters holds the attention of all.

> And when the living creatures give glory and honor and thanks to
> Him who sits on the throne, to Him who lives forever and ever, the
> twenty-four elders will fall down before Him who sits on the throne,
> and will worship Him who lives forever and ever, and will cast their
> crowns before the throne, saying,
> "Worthy are You, our Lord and our God, to receive glory
> and honor and power; for You created all things, and
> because of Your will they existed, and were created."
> (verses 9–11)

My friend, this is the worship being lavished right now at the feet of our Infinite God, the One who is worthy of our endless pursuit. The mighty angels have adored Him from eternity past. They were extolling His worth before time began, and they can't stop. This is our Creator, Redeemer, and Intimate Friend! He lives and breathes, and He won't fit in any compartment of our lives, regardless of how large a place we give Him or how nice and organized we keep our shrine. He isn't meant to be a part of our lives; He *is* our life.

> **This God Man isn't meant to be a part of our lives; He *is* our life.**

To never finish seeking God is to live the greatest adventure this life offers. You want a meaningful life? Take the challenge of Oswald Chambers: "Begin to know Him now, and finish never."[10]

THE DELICIOUS TRUTH THAT GIVES US A TASTE FOR MORE

Men and women have always craved miracles, and we always will. I believe God programmed us with a capacity for awe. What we are so much slower to understand is that Christ in us, living through us, is the miracle we most need to see.

"Show us a miracle and we'll believe," was the ancient cry of those we read about in the Bible, and human hearts repeat it today, whether shouted aloud by the atheist or murmured alone by the halting believer. We pine for miracles when all the while, God gave us one in Christ and made a way for us to become a miracle ourselves through the transforming power of that very gift: Christ in us, the hope of glory.

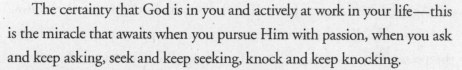

Christ in us, living through us,
is the miracle we most need to see.

The certainty that God is in you and actively at work in your life—this is the miracle that awaits when you pursue Him with passion, when you ask and keep asking, seek and keep seeking, knock and keep knocking.

Early in these pages I told you that although I had considered myself a believer for most of my life, my true journey in Christ started the day I stood singing "Oh, how I love Jesus" with a congregation of people and realized that I could just as easily have been singing "Oh, how I love watermelon." These days I thrill to know that I truly love Him and that He can read that truth in my heart like a poem shared between lovers. I can sing of this love to Him at the top of my lungs and be confident that, while the world may want earplugs in the worst way, my God is tapping His toe and enjoying the private concert.

And yet, here's the wonderful irony. My love for Jesus blossomed only after I became totally taken by the delicious truth that He loves me without reservation. And this is how He loves you.

"We love, because He first loved us" (1 John 4:19).

He loves us.

Understanding God's great love for us is where our ultimate satisfaction lies. Let the beauty of these words ever caress your grace-hungry heart.

> But when the kindness of God our Savior and His love for mankind appeared, He saved us, not on the basis of deeds which we have done in righteousness, but according to His mercy, by the washing of regeneration and renewing by the Holy Spirit, whom He poured out upon us richly through Jesus Christ our Savior, so that being justified by His grace we would be made heirs according to the hope of eternal life. (Titus 3:4–7)

Again, I need you to know that the prayers in this book aren't once-and-done steps I'm recommending to you from a past experiment. They're the present-tense, ongoing adventures of my life. The more He answers these prayers, the more earnestly I petition Him for more. I ask God to give me more love for Jesus, more courage to go further, higher, and deeper. I want more hunger for His Word, more awareness of Him in my days, more faith through a growing obedience born out of gratitude, more of Him and less of me, and more love for those with me on the journey. I'm always expressing my gratitude to Him for the fire that burns in my heart precisely because it once flickered so sporadically.

But I've found that these prayers, offered out of a heart desperate for more of Him, build on each other. His Word feeds me, and I want to spend more time with Him. When I spend more time with Him, I find myself wanting to please Him. When I yield in order to please Him, I become less self-conscious, more Christ-conscious. As a result I have more love for Him and for those around me.

And on and on and on He goes.

Chase Him Until He Catches You

Earlier in these pages I wondered aloud about why you may have picked up this book. Perhaps you have never made the decision to follow Christ and are curious. You're reading it because you have found yourself wondering more and more about Jesus. Then again, perhaps the title grabbed you because you're a believer who just flat out wants more from your faith. Whatever the reason that has brought us together in this moment, I have one last embarrassingly true story that seems tailor-made for these final thoughts.

I was a senior in high school when Phil the Blond graduated college and returned home to work on the family farm. At the time, my intentions were to leave our small town, become a journalist, and travel the world—but that fair-haired boy in the big blue farm truck caught my eye! Before long I had adjusted my sights. Phil was smack-dab in the cross hairs of my future plans.

Of course, I was smooth, liquid smooth. I let Phil think that he was chasing me, while I did all the things a smart belle does to make sure I was standing wherever he was looking. I went out of my way to show up on his radar, and then I slowed down long enough to get noticed. It seemed all my friends knew of my growing crush. One afternoon, a buddy of mine told me that Phil planned to attend my basketball game that evening. I was one nervous Nellie, but I was equally determined to make a lasting impression. And I did, just not in the way I had planned.

Halfway through the game my Phil radar went off, alerting me that he was in the vicinity. Sure enough, the object of my affections was standing at the far end of the gym. This was my moment. If ever there was a time to be an impressive athlete, this was it. I ratcheted up my defense. Before long I had actually stolen the ball and was headed full speed toward our goal, hoping that my breakaway lay-up would capture his attention.

I succeeded.

With the whole gym watching, I dribbled the ball right off the toes of my big fat feet! I watched as it rolled all the way down the floor to where my crush was standing. Phil picked it up, returned it to the referee, and looked my way. My face was as red as the numbers on my uniform, but I turned on the charm anyway and gave the boy my biggest, brightest smile. Forgive me for mixing sports analogies, but from that moment on it was game, set, match! By the time Phil got around to asking Papa for my hand, I was already thinking of names for our unborn children.

Friend, you may have thought you were acting on a whim when you picked up this book, but it was no accident. Whatever stimulated your interest, the yearning didn't originate with you. You're in God's cross hairs as surely as that blond-headed boy was in mine. What you're feeling is the Holy Spirit wooing you to the Father.

Let me ask you a question. Have you ever felt good and lonely? I have. The feeling can assail us at the strangest times and has nothing whatsoever to do with other people. We can feel good and lonely in a crowd. Being good and lonely doesn't exactly make us sad; it just fills us with a tender, sweet longing.

Friend, I believe good and lonely is our heart reaching for home. The next one. The eternal one. As Hebrews 11:16 says of the heroes of faith who preceded us, "They were longing for a better country—a heavenly one. Therefore God is not ashamed to be called their God, for he has prepared a city for them" (NIV).

God doesn't want to be the Great Spectator of our lives. He desires to live life with us, in us, and through us, and then to take us home when all is said and done. Far from being a party pooper, our Father wants to see us enjoy our lives and make merry. He just wants us to make merry over the right thing, over the Real Thing.

His name is Jesus.

BIBLE STUDY AND DISCUSSION GUIDE

The following questions are designed to take you just a little further in your pursuit of All Things Jesus. You'll find a handful of questions for each chapter, followed by a short wrap-up from me and a prompt to lead you into conversation with God. Whether you're working through this study guide on your own or with a group, first read the pertinent chapter, then grab your Bible, a notebook, and a pen so you can write down your answers and record your personal prayers.

Chapter 1: When All You Can Bring Him Is a Broken Want-To

1. Read Mark 12:13–34. In this passage of Scripture we find Jesus being questioned by the religious leaders of the Jews. According to verse 13, what was their goal?

2. In verse 28 we read of one scribe who had been carefully observing this inquisition. What question did he pose to Jesus, and what answer did he receive in response?

3. On a scale of 1 to 10, with 1 representing "I believe in God" and 10 representing "I passionately love this God," where do you think you stand in regard to the foremost or Greatest Commandment?

4. Carefully read the scribe's rephrasing of Jesus's answer in verses 32–33. What did Jesus say in verse 34 about the state of this man's heart?

5. Read Acts 17:26–28. What does the second half of verse 27 tell us about where God is?

———

The Jews wanted one big hang-your-hat-on-it rule. Jesus gave them one big rest-on-it remedy that was as near to them as the words on their lips. Love God, love others. Bam! Don't pursue law. Pursue love.

The scribe knew that loving God was more important than all the sacrifices, traditions, and rules of their religious system. Had he combined that knowledge with a determination to pursue such a love for God, we might have seen him again in the Scriptures. As it is, we don't know if he discovered that passion. We only know he could have. Jesus said he was close to the kingdom of God.

Ours is a God who is near (see Jeremiah 23:23). Regardless of where you put yourself on that scale of 1 to 10, He is close. Let the truth of His nearness encourage you today.

Pursue Him in Prayer
Write out your prayer of commitment to pursue Him with the full expectation that He will meet you in the chase.

CHAPTER 2: COURAGE FOR US NOT-SO-SUPER SAINTS

1. Describe at least one area of your faith walk where you need more courage.

2. Read Hebrews 12:1–3. Courage doesn't mean we don't feel fear; it means we know how to carry on despite it. What does verse 3 say we should be doing while Jesus, the Author of our faith, is perfecting it? What does that admonition mean to you in your own words?

3. Describe a time when the presence of another person helped you face your fears.

4. Even if they want to, people can't always be there for us, but our God is forever faithful. Read Psalm 90:1–2. What does this passage call Him?

5. Read John 14:15–21. How does an understanding of God's faithfulness prepare your heart to obey Him out of love rather than fear?

The writer of Psalm 118:6 said, "The LORD is on my side; I will not fear" (NKJV). I don't believe he was declaring that he would never again feel fear or intimidation. I think he was saying that when faced with such fear he would take courage in the God who promised to never leave him or forsake him.

As believers, we have the abiding presence of God in our lives through the gift of the Holy Spirit, the One who lives in us as our Helper (see John 14:26). Our confidence in Him grows when we look in the face of whatever intimidates us and choose to draw on His fresh, renewable courage over and over again.

Pursue Him in Prayer

Write out a prayer asking God to help you recognize intimidation in its various forms and turn to the Holy Spirit for courage every time to press past them all.

CHAPTER 3: I SUPPOSE CLIFFSNOTES ARE OUT

1. What is the greatest challenge you face when it comes to spending time in the Bible?

2. Read John 17. In this chapter, known as the high priestly prayer, Jesus prayed for all believers, those who received His words and believed in Him in His day and those who would believe in the future. What did Jesus ask the Father to do in verse 17? What means did He say God would use to accomplish this?

3. To sanctify something means to set it apart or devote it for sacred use. All believers are set apart unto God, but Jesus tied the process of our becoming increasingly sanctified and devoted for sacred use with the ongoing revelation of truth. In John 14:26 who did Jesus promise would come to help us understand His teachings?

4. What do you see in Psalm 119:26–27 that hints at how each of us can cooperate in the teaching process?

5. In John 17:18 what did Jesus reveal as one of His reasons for enrolling His followers in this divine continuing-education course?

———

Jesus doesn't want to take believers out of the world, and He doesn't want us to blend in with it; He wants us to change the world. We can't do this and we won't until we are first transformed ourselves. This doesn't happen automatically when we come to Jesus. That's the message of Romans 12:2: "And do not be conformed to this world, but be transformed by the renewing of your mind, so that you may prove what the will of God is, that which is good and acceptable and perfect."

This transformation and renewal of our minds occurs as we behold the glory of the Lord, especially as revealed in the Bible. As D. L. Moody once said, "Let the Word of God into your soul, and it will inspire you. It can not help it."[11]

Pursue Him in Prayer

Read 2 Corinthians 3:18 and write out a prayer expressing your commitment to read the Word and asking the Holy Spirit to teach you the truths of Jesus and transform you through them.

CHAPTER 4: DOES GOD WANT OUT OF OUR QUIET TIMES?

1. How would you describe your current prayer life? What, if anything, would you like to change about it, and why?

2. Read 1 Thessalonians 5:16–18. Beginning with verse 16, record the three precepts or practices that the writer challenges each of us to follow. Underline the middle one.

3. To understand how we can pray without ceasing, we should find out what it doesn't mean. Read Matthew 6:5–8 and Mark 12:38–40. In your own words, what kind of praying did Jesus warn His listeners against?

4. Now read Philippians 4:4–9. What are we told to do always in verse 4, and according to verse 6, what are we to do in everything?

5. Sandwiched between those admonitions is verse 5. Write it down.

———

Did you see the similarity between our verses from Philippians and 1 Thessalonians? Choosing joy and giving thanks helps us develop the type of ongoing conversation with God that we're craving and transforms our perspective on our circumstances.

To pray unceasingly is to cultivate and nurture a growing appreciation for the presence of God and His abiding presence that will not only be a blessing to us, but also bless those around us.

Pursue Him in Prayer
Write out your commitment to seek the constant awareness of God in your daily routine.

CHAPTER 5: ARE SOME OF US STUCK WITH MESSED-UP MUSTARD SEEDS?

1. Read the third chapter of Genesis. According to verses 23–24, what happened to Adam and Eve as a result of disobeying God?

2. The Creator's intention to live among the created would not be thwarted indefinitely. Read Exodus 25:8. What did God instruct the nation of Israel to build and for what purpose?

3. Read Deuteronomy 6:24–25. What does verse 24 reveal about the reasons for obeying God's commands, and what does verse 25 promise us as a result of keeping them?

4. Read Romans 8:3–4. What persistent problem does this passage identify, and what solution does it celebrate?

5. Read 1 Corinthians 6:19–20. Where is God's temple located today? How should that knowledge shape your choices?

From the beginning of recorded time and all the way through Scripture, we see Holy God desiring to walk among His people and be their God. We can also see disobedience denying man the privilege of God's presence, over and over again. Into this cycle of defeat came the Hope of Glory. John 1:14 says the Word of God became flesh and dwelt—"tabernacled" or "pitched His tent"—among us in the body of His Son, Jesus the Messiah. Those who believe in Jesus are set right with God and given the indescribable gift of His Spirit to dwell in us on earth.

The Spirit of God that lives in believers today is the same God who walked in the garden with Adam and Eve. Disobedience still grieves Him. Obedience forever delights Him.

Pursue Him in Prayer
Write out a prayer declaring your intentions to yield to Him and grow in grace and truth.

CHAPTER 6: WE ARE ALWAYS ON OUR MIND

1. What are some of the things we tend to obsess over when our eyes are on ourselves?

2. Read Matthew 11:28. What promise does Jesus make here, and what must we do to secure it?

3. Self-consciousness and introspection can lead us down paths of despair and discouragement. Only walking with Jesus leads to rest. Based on Matthew 11:29–30, what is the evidence that we're yoked to the sweet grace of Jesus and not trying to follow Him in our own efforts?

4. Read Psalm 116:7. What did the psalmist remind himself of when he needed to find rest for his troubled soul?

5. What truth could you take from this chapter to remember the next
time you find yourself knee-deep in a self-examination?

———

Self-examination, whether spiritual or physical, always leads us away from
the sweet abiding consciousness of the Spirit's presence. If we think we're
"doing pretty good," we'll miss Jesus by a country mile. If we decide we're
"doing poorly," we'll miss Him by an equal distance.

I've found that it is literally impossible to focus on self while simultaneously celebrating the glory of Jesus, my blessed Substitute, who has given
me such eternal favor in the Father's eyes. Thinking of Him frees me from
the bothersome weight of evaluating me.

Pursue Him in Prayer

In your own words, write out a request that the Lord will help you be quick
to realize when you need to turn your eyes back to Him.

CHAPTER 7: MAY WE HAVE PERMISSION
TO SLAP 'EM SILLY IN JESUS'S NAME?

1. Describe a time when a fellow believer showed you grace and love
when you didn't deserve it.

2. Read Psalm 133. What two metaphors did the writer use to describe what it's like for God's people to dwell together in unity?

3. Consider the sweet fragrance of the first metaphor. How might that describe the appeal to those around us when believers are in agreement as opposed to when we are fractious and disagreeable?

4. Now consider the second metaphor, described in verse 3. What effect does dew have on the grass, and how would that relate to what happens to believers dwelling in unity?

5. Read Psalm 133 once more, paying close attention to the last verse. What does the Lord do when He finds such unity?

Oh, I need to testify! This manuscript was written first, and the study guide came afterward. As I neared the end I suddenly felt inexplicably and unexpectedly weary. I picked up my phone to send a group text to a few of my Jesus-loving girlfriends, asking for prayer support. As I tapped out the message, I found my eyes filling with tears. Being female, I'm quite used to crying for no apparent reason, but I was still surprised by the sudden surge of emotion. It was only after I hit Send and returned to my work that I saw the connection between where I was and why the Holy Spirit prompted me to reach out to those I call my Warrior Women. I was here, in this section on the body of Christ.

How desperately we need each other. How precious He was to remind me.

Pursue Him in Prayer

Please write out a prayer of appreciation for those who journey with you as you seek to know Jesus more fully and love Him more deeply. They are not silver, dear one; they are gold.

CHAPTER 8: TILL WE SEE HIM FACE TO FACE

1. Describe a time when you felt good and lonely. How did God meet you in that moment?

2. Read Proverbs 4:18. None of us is exempt from trouble in this life, but if we follow the path God has set out for us, what does this verse say we can expect to happen?

3. What is the benefit of having light on your path, and what does it mean to you that your path will grow brighter and brighter?

4. In what ways have you been challenged by *Heart Wide Open*? What specific changes have you experienced or chosen as a result of what you've read?

5. Look back at your answer to question 3 in the Bible study for chapter 1. Would your answer be different today? If so, explain why.

Pursue Him in Prayer

Record your prayer of commitment to continue chasing after God until you reach your eternal home.

*D*ear reader, thank you for reading *Heart Wide Open.* I consider it a privilege to walk this journey alongside you, and I would be honored to take your prayer requests before the throne. I invite you to share them with me at tomtom@allthingssouthern.com.

–Shellie

ACKNOWLEDGMENTS

When *Heart Wide Open* was nothing more than an untitled and fuzzy dream, my agent, Greg Johnson at WordServe Literary, and his wife, Becky, lunched, laughed, and brainstormed with me until something akin to substance surfaced that I could take home and nurture. Thank you both.

Editor extraordinaire Laura Barker did more than adopt my baby into the WaterBrook Multnomah family. She took *Heart Wide Open* into her own. Without you, Laura, my baby would've gone into the world half-naked and malnourished. Thank you for going above and beyond.

To the entire team at WaterBrook Multnomah, thank you for working so hard to get *Heart Wide Open* on the shelves and in the hands of booksellers and potential readers!

To Jonathan and Amy Wiggins from Resurrection Fellowship in Loveland, Colorado, thank you for buying into the message of *Heart Wide Open* and making yourselves and your congregation available to spread it. To Calvary Baptist Church in Bainbridge, Georgia, and Midland Baptist Church in Jena, Louisiana, thank you for being willing "guinea pigs."

To my Pastor and his wife, Brother Don and Mrs. Linda, thank you for shepherding me and mine so well all these years.

To the Warrior Women of Providence Church, thank you for the prayer support!

To my "friends of the thin place," Rhonda Perry and Nicole Seitz, thank you for helping me hear the voice of our Beloved.

To Papa and Nance, thank you for the priceless heritage of believing parents. To my sisters, thank you for being friends too. To my kids and grandkids, thanks for loving this "Keggie" so well, despite my stranger-than-your-average-bear ways.

To my darling husband, who endlessly supports the countless hours spent at the screen and on the road. Phil Tomlinson, all I can give you is a line of your own, but we both know your name should be on every cover!

Above all, to my sweet Jesus, thank You for saving my soul and teaching me what it means to live in delicious desperation for Your abiding presence. Only You know how often I swing between "Whatever made me think I could do this?" and "There just may be the slightest chance I'm getting my message across." Thank You for those three words You gave me on one of my worst doubting days. I've clung to those golden words as if they were a life preserver: "Trust the team." Thank You for surrounding me with wise and talented people to help make sense of the words pouring from my wide open heart. Your team rocks! Help me to love You with everything in me for all of my days.

—Shellie Rushing Tomlinson

NOTES

1. Dictionary.com, s.v. "hypocrite," http://dictionary.reference.com/browse/hypocrite.

2. C. H. Spurgeon, *Morning and Evening: Daily Readings,* complete and unabridged, New Modern edition, (Peabody, MA: Hendrickson, 2006), April 26, morning.

3. See for example Matthew 9:2; 9:22; 14:27; Mark 6:50; John 16:33.

4. The Free Dictionary, s.v. "exercise," www.thefreedictionary.com/exercise.

5. J. H. Sammis, "Trust and Obey," 1887, public domain.

6. Henry David Thoreau, *Walden,* vol. 2 (Boston: Houghton Mifflin, 1892), 502.

7. The NAS New Testament Greek Lexicon, Bible Study Tools, s.v. "dokimazo," www.biblestudytools.com/lexicons/greek/nas/dokimazo.html.

8. Chad Owen Brand et al., eds., *Holman Illustrated Bible Dictionary* (Nashville: B&H, 2003), 200.

9. The Free Dictionary, s.v. "Achilles' heel," www.thefreedictionary.com/Achilles'+heel.

10. Oswald Chambers, *My Utmost for His Highest: Selections for the Year* (Grand Rapids, MI: Oswald Chambers Publications and Marshall Pickering, 1986), May 27.

11. D. L. Moody, *Pleasure and Profit in Bible Study* (New York: Revell, 1895), 26.